The
WISDOM
of
THE ARABS

The
WISDOM
of
THE ARABS

Compiled by Suheil Bushrui

ONEWORLD

OXFORD

THE WISDOM OF THE ARABS

Oneworld Publications
(Sales and Editorial)
185 Banbury Road
Oxford OX2 7AR
England
www.oneworld-publications.com

© Oneworld 2002

ISBN 1–85168–283–X

Cover and text design by Design Deluxe
Typeset by LaserScript Limited, Mitcham, UK
Printed and bound by Graphicom Srl, Vicenza, Italy

Speaking the Greek's own language, just because
Your Greek eludes you, leave the least of flaws
In contracts with him; while, since Arab lore
Holds the stars' secret – take one trouble more
And master it!

SORDELLO, BOOK IV, R. Browning

I have read, reverend Fathers, in the works of the
Arabs, that when Abdala the Saracen was asked
what he regarded as most to be wondered at on the
world's stage, so to speak, he answered that there
was nothing to be seen more wonderful than man.

ORATIO DE DIGNITATE HOMINIS, Giovanni Pico. Della Mirandola

CONTENTS

INTRODUCTION

At the beginning of the seventh century CE, the world witnessed with astonishment the emergence of a great civilization from the heart of the Arabian Peninsula. It rapidly developed into an extraordinary attempt by a single people to unify the known world under the banner of its own language, culture and religion.

The forces that had shaped the ancient world had largely left the Arabs untouched. But in the seventh century, time and place strategically positioned them to borrow and derive full benefit from the great civilizations around them. They stamped everything they received with their genius, and at the same time made their own unique contribution to human civilization. Suddenly a new breed of men, extraordinarily subtle, vital and intelligent, opened their hearts and minds to all nations and invited others everywhere to join in the unique enterprise of fashioning a spiritually oriented civil society. They were spurred by an insatiable appetite for secular and divine knowledge and spared no effort to profit from the wisdom and experience of others, in whatever quarter these might be found. In the East, they found inspiration in the spiritual profundity of Persian and Indian mysticism and the down-to-earth simplicity of Chinese philosophy. In the West, they benefited from the surviving vestiges of ancient Egypt and revived through their researches the intellectual heritage of Greece and Rome. In the South-west, they interacted with the early civilizations of Africa. At the height of their glory they were able to build a cosmopolitan civilization unsurpassed in richness and diversity by any that had preceded it.

Whether by instinct or temperament, the Arabs were primarily a poetic people – a characteristic that has been preserved to this very day. A marked oral literary tradition appears to have accompanied them from the earliest period of their development. Like the Irish, the Arabs have a passion for the spoken word, the gracious turn of phrase, the simple but inimitably elegant expression. Poetry formed indeed their soul: the essence of their literature; a record of their history, their traditions, their genealogy; and at all times a chronicle of their conflicts, wars and reconciliations, as well as a measure of their love for life, for women and for the world at large. Yet by virtue of this same genius they yearned, too, for a world beyond the present, and so their Sufi bards sang the songs of divine love, kindling the mystic fires of yearning for reunion with God. Their poetic gift expressed itself in every possible form: the panegyric, the elegy, the eulogy, the fable, the hunt and love poems. Poetry for them was life; while life was most fully expressed in poetry. The great poets Al-Mutannabí and Abu'l-'Alá' Al-Ma'arrí stand shoulder to shoulder with Europe's finest lyricists, such as Shakespeare, Goethe and Dante. For it has been wisely remarked, 'Among the poets there is no competition in the Kingdom of God.'

Within the bounds of their homeland, the Arabs were spiritualized and ennobled by the birth of Islam and the great Revelation enshrined in its Most Holy Book, the Qur'án. It was progressively vouchsafed to the Prophet Muhammad throughout His Ministry and thereafter exerted incalculable influence on all aspects of Arab life. Its importance was not confined to the religious, moral and philosophical dimensions, for it furnished a model of matchless eloquence and became also the ultimate criterion of literary accomplishment in Arabic. Over successive generations the Islamic Revelation instilled into the Arabs an innate appreciation of 'books' – these conceived as repositories of liberal learning in the broadest sense – and an instinctive reverence for the 'Word'. Informing as it does their whole literary tradition, this peculiar veneration of the 'Word' manifests itself even in their chosen modes of expression, genres and literary forms. The Arabs have a special predilection for sententious utterances of all kinds, which finds expression in proverb, allegory, prose epigram, aphorism, adage, apothegm, parable, didactic story, fable, and a vast body of folk literary traditions.

A combination of cultural, spiritual and scientific achievements ushered in the Arab world's golden age. For nearly half a millennium from the tenth to the fourteenth centuries CE, Arab dynasties reigned over far-stretching regions of the earth – territories exceeded in extent only by the Roman Empire at its height. Among the particular glories of this period were the cities of Baghdad, Cairo and Cordova – the Arab cultural capitals respectively of the Asian, African and European continents. They became renowned for their great libraries and institutions of higher learning, and illuminated surrounding territories and regions far beyond with the profoundly humanizing values imparted by the nascent Islamic civilization. In every branch of learning the Arabs made remarkable and enduring contributions that may justly be regarded as laying the foundation for the European Renaissance and, accordingly, for the modern world. In his three-volume *Introduction to the History of Science*, George Sarton has observed that for no less than seven hundred years the world's greatest scholars in numerous fields of inquiry were Arabs.

Elevated as the tongue of Revelation by Islam, Arabic became one of the foremost languages of learning. Its incalculable precision, subtlety and flexibility made it the ideal instrument for assimilating and transmitting the accumulated learning of a wide range of diverse cultures. It became the repository of the wisdom of the ages, the storehouse wherein were gathered the fairest fruits of human enlightenment from the far-flung arc of knowledge extending across the heart of two continents, from the Pacific coast of China to the Atlantic shores of the Iberian Peninsula. Vast as was the area under the Arabs' temporal sway, it was exceeded by the immense range of their intellectual dominion. The boundaries of the former did not surpass the confines of China, the southern limits of the Sahara, and the northern plains of Europe, but the empire of the latter extended into the furthest reaches of the then-known world. The harmony of civilizations effected by the Arabs reached its zenith in Andalusia – the name they gave to Spain. Among the outstanding features of their noble and distinctive achievements was their contribution to that whole corpus of universally accepted truths and values known as the 'perennial philosophy', which has, to this day, remained a living tradition. That 'perennial wisdom' is the 'eternal wisdom' of all ages, shared and developed by all humanity.

Principles of selection and identification

To compile an anthology on the theme 'wisdom of the Arabs' is to have borne in upon one that the literature in question expresses in essence the same 'perennial philosophy' or 'eternal wisdom' that forms the common heritage of all races, albeit seen from their own unique perspective. In any such endeavour a central dilemma inevitably arises: what to adopt as the criterion of selection? The difficulty is compounded here by the sheer bulk of Arabic literature; but this is offset by the comparatively much smaller volume of translations available in English. Fortunately, a good number of the most eminent Arab authors have been introduced to the English-speaking world, and their works made available by at least one gifted translator, so that what might seem a truly formidable undertaking is reduced in fact to the much more feasible, though still sufficiently demanding, task of making judicious selections from a limited number of well-known works in reputable translations.

Notwithstanding the inherent interest and importance of the subject, the present anthology marks the first attempt in modern times to present in English translation a representative collection of extracts illustrating the Arabic 'perennial philosophy'. The volume encompasses a broad spectrum of different approaches and styles of translation that evolved over a period of some three hundred years from the eighteenth century to the present day – a period during which the considerable interest taken by the English-speaking world in all aspects of the 'Orient' under its Ottoman suzerains formed the most significant stimulus for this activity. Such interest, however, represented but a resurgence of the same fruitful interaction with Arab culture that had sustained the intellectual life of Europe during its Dark Ages. It is indeed noteworthy that the first book ever printed in England, by William Caxton in 1477 during the reign of Edward IV, itself bears witness to this connection. The book, entitled *The Dictes and Wise Saying of the Philosophers*, was translated by Earl Rivers from a French translation of a Latin rendering of an originally Arabic work by Abu'l-Wafá' Mubashshir Ibn Fátik entitled *Mukhtár al-Hikam*, itself a compilation of the wisdom of the Greek philosophers published in Egypt in the eleventh century.

The contents of the present work are of two categories: the first comprises passages excerpted from other sources and reproduced in their original form (preserving idiosyncrasies of spelling, orthography and verse arrangement) without accompanying footnotes, which were deemed unnecessary in this context. Notwithstanding the existence in various passages of certain slight obscurities, I have still felt it preferable not to detract from their integrity by burdening the reader with unnecessary explanations. The second category comprises passages from the vast corpus of so-far untranslated materials – passages that have particularly impressed me in my own travels through these 'realms of gold', and which I accordingly present here in translations of my own.

Should the anthology appear to pass over materials that might have been thought worthy of inclusion, I can only plead in excuse that no such compilation can ever satisfy all tastes and that many seeming omissions were in any case quite deliberate. From the twentieth century I have confined myself to selections from Kahlil Gibran and Ameen Rihani, the two most prominent and internationally recognized Arab authors of the time. Additional material that could not be included in the published version of this book can be found online at www.bsos.umd.edu/cidcm/gibran/. Follow the link for 'publications' and click on *The Wisdom of the Arabs*.

As regards the layout of the compilation, the excerpts have been accompanied by just so much explanation as has been felt necessary to enhance appreciation of their merits without altering the character of a work intended for the general reader. Below each passage the name of the author, when known, is provided, followed by the name of the translator, identified merely as 'Editor' in the case of passages newly rendered by myself. Sayings, statements and aphorisms forming part of common parlance are designated generically as 'folk traditions', rather than assigned to a particular source. Cases where the translator is unknown are labelled 'Anonymous'. For ease of identification the titles of famous works, such as *The Arabian Nights* and *Kalila and Dimna*, are consistently presented, even should they be given differently in the parent source. A full bibliography of all the various sources consulted in compiling this anthology is appended at the end of the volume.

A NOTE ON TRANSLATION AND TRANSLITERATION

On Translation

The chief part of this anthology is accounted for by extracts from Arabic poetry – the form that best encapsulates the spirit of the race. In this regard, it may be noted that there scarcely exists a more exacting creative activity than that of rendering poetry from one language into another. The problems encountered are as numerous as they are intractable and were eloquently expressed more than a millennium ago by the foremost master of Arabic prose, Abu 'Uthmán 'Umar Ibn Bahr Al-Jáhiz (775–868 CE), whose inquiry into the perplexity of such an undertaking led him in fact to advise against its being attempted at all:

> Poetry cannot be translated, nor should it be paraphrased, for once so transported its order is disrupted, its metre fractured, its beauty lost, its points of novelty and delight devalued, and it becomes as ordinary prose.

More generally, however, the task of translating Arabic into English – whether involving poetry or prose – is one notoriously fraught with difficulty. Some poetic translations convey the gist and purport of the original while disregarding aspects of form, rhyme and metre; others, though academically 'worthy', lack grace and elegance and indefinably misrepresent the spirit of the text. Few indeed follow successfully a middle course so as to become faithful renderings in the fullest sense.

The various formidable obstacles enumerated by Al-Jáhiz as standing in the way of translating poetry are hardly less applicable to the task of translating prose. Undoubtedly the best results have been obtained by those translators who are not only steeped in the language and culture of the Arabs, but have also a gift of fluent and lyrical expression in English that enables them masterfully to convey, on the basis of a proper understanding, both the formal and the spiritual elements of any given piece. Each fine translation represents a landmark in the age and cultural milieu in which it was composed; each such translation marks, too, an interpretive effort of the first order, resulting in a new creation which then assumes a life and legitimacy of its own.

On Transliteration

In discussing different systems of transliteration, the controversial English Arabist Richard Francis Burton offered a conclusion that has informed my own work:

> As regards the transliteration of Arabic words I deliberately reject the artful and complicated system, ugly and clumsy withal, affected by scientific modern Orientalists ... the devices perplex the simple and teach nothing to the learned.

In fact, the transliteration of Arabic names and terms is still an area of some confusion. Considerable divergences obtain between one translator and the next, as may indeed be judged even from the extracts assembled in this volume. This notwithstanding, certain preferences are lately gaining prevalence – 'Qur'án', for example, in the place of the traditional 'Koran', a spelling redolent of the prejudicial attitude with which Islam had for many centuries been viewed. I have adopted such accepted forms where available and have had recourse in other cases to a simple system of my own creation, which seeks above all to replicate the pronunciation of the original Arabic. In line with this approach I have limited myself in distinguishing the Arabic orthography of transliterated terms to the apostrophe and the inverted comma: ['] for the Arabic glottal stop Hamzah, [ء] and ['] for the Arabic consonant 'Ayn [ع]. Further to reproduce the Arabic phonetic system, so distinct from that of English, would, I feel, have resulted in a distracting and unwarranted proliferation of diacritical symbols. As for transliterations in the quoted texts, these I have left exactly as they appeared in the sources from which they were extracted.

DIVINE PATH

GOD

IN THE name of God, Most Gracious, Most Merciful.
Praise be to God,
The Cherisher and Sustainer of the Worlds;
Most Gracious, Most Merciful;
Master of the Day of Judgment.
Thee do we worship,
And Thine aid we seek.
Show us the straight way,
The way of those on whom
Thou has bestowed Thy Grace,
Those whose (portion)
Is not wrath,
And who go not astray.

QUR'AN 1: 1–7

GOD IS the Light
Of the heavens and the earth.

QUR'AN 24: 35

IT IS He Who brings out
The living from the dead,
And brings out the dead
From the living, and Who
Gives life to the earth.

GOD SAITH, 'The person I hold as a beloved, I am his hearing by which he heareth, and I am his sight by which he seeth, and I am his hands by which he holdeth, and I am his feet by which he walketh.'

HADITH

TO ACT ethically in the spirit of service to God will only occur when four qualities come together: fear of God, hope, love and certainty.

AL-'AMERI, *Editor*

Thus you may know that the existing things are of two classes: universal things and part-things. The universal things start with the most accomplished ones, and then [come] the lower and lower ones, down to the lowest among them. They form nine degrees of which the first among them, who is the foremost one, is (1) the Creator – He is Highly Exalted – who is the cause of all. Then [comes] (2) the Mind, then (3) the Soul, then (4) the Nature, then (5) the First Matter, then (6) the Absolute Body, then (7) the Celestial Sphere, then (8) the Four Elements, and then (9) the three Compositions, which are the last of them.

Ikhwan Al-Safa, *Widengren*

If God desires to be united with a servant of His, He opens to him the gate of worship, and if he delights in worship, He opens to him the gate of proximity, then He raises him to the station of fellowship, then He seats him on the throne of unification.

Abu Sa'id Ahmad Ibn 'Isa al-Kharraz, *Smith*

O SON of Adam! Fear not the mighty and powerful as long as my dominion prevails, for my dominion has no end.

O son of Adam! Fret not in the face of poverty as long as my treasures are replenished, for my treasures are inexhaustible.

O son of Adam! Do not seek the company of others as long as I am your friend, for if you seek me you shall find me, but if you seek others I shall forsake you and you shall forfeit all bounty.

FOLK TRADITION, *Editor*

A SLAVE who accepts the will of God is a freeman but a freeman who is obsessed by ambition is a slave.

FOLK TRADITION, *Editor*

IN ALL matters rely on God the Compassionate,
For he who relies on Him never fails.
Trust God and be resigned to His will;
Your need of Him, He shall then fulfill.

FOLK TRADITION, *Editor*

REFRAIN FROM seeking to understand God and be satisfied to recognize His bounties.

FOLK TRADITION, *Editor*

EVERYTHING IN the world is derived from the Light of His Essence and all beauty and perfection are the gift of His bounty, and to attain fully to this illumination is salvation.

SHIHAB AL-DIN SUHRAWARDI HALABI AL-MAQTUL, *Smith*

DIVINE LOVE is God's love for us; our love for God may also be called Divine. Spiritual love is that which desires to please the beloved; it serves no desire and has no will of its own, but serves the beloved for his own sake.

IBN 'ARABI, *Editor*

THE VOICE OF THE SUFI

To BE a Sufi means to abide continuously in God and to live at peace with men: whoever abides in God and deals rightly with men, treating them with unfailing kindness, is a Sufi.

AL-GHAZZALI, *Smith*

IT IS through him [The Perfect Man] that God looks at His creatures and dispenses His Mercy upon them; for he is the adventitious man, and yet he has no beginning; he is ephemeral and yet he is everlastingly eternal. He is also the Word which divides and unites. The world subsists in virtue of his existence. He is to the world what the setting of a seal is to the seal: that is to say the place where the imprint is engraved, the symbol with which the king seals his treasures. This is why he has been called *khalifa*: for through him God preserves His creation, as the seal preserves the treasures. As long as the king's seal remains unbroken, no one would dare to open the treasures without his permission. Thus Man has been charged to guard the kingdom, and the world will be preserved for as long as the Perfect Man subsists therein.

IBN AL-'ARABI, *Sherrad*

TRUE AFFECTION between two people is never a reality unless each addresses the other by the pronoun 'I'.

FOLK TRADITION, *Editor*

THE PERSON who wears wool [the Sufi] must be the purest person of his age, the best person in morals, the noblest of humankind in his actions, the sweetest person in his nature, the most generous of them in spirit, and the most open-handed in his liberality. Just as he is distinguished from humanity in general by his clothing, he must also be distinguished from them in his spiritual characteristics.

AMAT AL-'AZIZ, *Cornell*

O GOD! if I worship Thee in fear of Hell, burn me in Hell; and if I worship Thee in hope of Paradise, exclude me from Paradise; but if I worship Thee for Thine own sake, withhold not Thine Everlasting Beauty!

RABI'A AL-'ADAWIYYA, *Arberry*

THOU ART my life and the innermost secret of my heart;
Wherever I am, there also art thou ...

AL-HALLAJ, *Editor*

I LOOKED one day at the Light and I did not cease looking at it
until I became the Light.

AL-NURI, *Smith*

I CRY to You for signs that have been gathered up by
intellects;
Nothing now remains of them in books except debris.

AL-HALLAJ, *Mason*

WHEN THE gnostic's spiritual eye is opened, his bodily eye is shut:
he sees nothing but God.

SUFI MAXIM, *Nicholson*

SUFISM IS enmity to this world and friendship with the Lord.

AL-NURI, *Smith*

I SAW my Lord with the eye of my heart. I asked: 'Who art thou?',
   He said: 'I am thou'.

AL-HALLAJ, Editor

WHEN THE heart weeps because it has lost, the spirit laughs
   because it has found.

SUFI MAXIM, Nicholson

MY LOVE for God leaves no room for hating Satan.

RABI'A AL-'ADAWIYYA, Smith

MY LOVE for my Lord
Consumes and makes me weak.
How can I say to Him,
It is Your doing.

AL-HALLAJ, Mason

TWO WAYS I love Thee: selfishly,
And next, as worthy is of Thee.
'Tis selfish love that I do naught
Save think on Thee with every thought;
'Tis purest love when Thou dost raise
The veil to my adoring gaze.

RABI'A AL-'ADAWIYYA, Nicholson

I AM He whom I love and He whom I love is I;
We are two souls dwelling in one body.
When you look at me you can see Him,
And you can see us both when you look at Him.

AL-HALLAJ, Badawi

MY HEART is capable of every form:
A cloister for the monk, a fane for idols,
A pasture for gazelles, the votary's Ka'ba,
The tables of the Torah, the Koran.
Love is the faith I hold: wherever turn
His camels, still the one true faith is mine.

IBN 'ARABI, Nicholson

The Voice of the Sufi ✽ 31

WITH MY Beloved I alone have been
When secrets tenderer than evening airs
Passed, and the Vision blest
Was granted to my prayers,
That crowned me, else obscure, with endless fame,
The while amazed between
His beauty and His majesty
I stood in silent ecstasy,
Revealing that which o'er my spirit went and came.
Lo, in His face commingled
Is every charm and grace;
The whole of Beauty singled
Into a perfect face
Beholding Him would cry,
'There is no God but He, and He is the most High!'

IBN AL-FARID, *Nicholson*

RIGHTEOUSNESS, PIETY AND HOLY LIFE

IT IS not righteousness
That ye turn your faces
Towards East or West;
But it is righteousness –
To believe in God
And the Last Day,
And the Angels,
And the Book,
And the Messengers;
To spend of your substance,
Out of love for Him,
For your kin,
For orphans,
For the needy,
For the wayfarer,
For those who ask,
And for the ransom of slaves;
To be steadfast in prayer,
And practice regular charity;
To fulfil the contracts
Which ye have made;

And to be firm and patient,
In pain (or suffering)
And adversity,
And throughout
All periods of panic.
Such are the people
Of truth, the God-fearing.

QUR'AN 2: 177

THOSE WHO believe (in the Qur'an),
Those who follow the Jewish (scriptures),
And the Sabians and the Christians, –
Any who believe in God
And the Last Day,
And work righteousness, –
On them shall be no fear,
Nor shall they grieve.

QUR'AN 5: 72

VERILY NEVER
Will God change the condition
Of a people until they
Change it themselves.

QUR'AN 13: 11

THE THREE qualities of jealousy, greed, and cupidity are innate in the sons of Adam until the Day of Judgement: the wise suppress them, the ignorant display them.

FOLK TRADITION, Editor

UNION WITH God requires the servant to achieve four states which are also called stations; the first is the station of the righteous, which is achieved through fear [of God]; the second is the station of the beneficent, which is achieved through hope; the third is the station of the pious, which is achieved through love; the fourth is the station of the devout, which is achieved through sincerity – but steadfastness is the essence of each one of these stations.

AL-'AMERI, Editor

KNOW THAT the beginning of guidance is outward piety and the end of guidance is inward piety.

AL-GHAZZALI, *Watt*

A BEDOUIN who had reached a hundred and twenty five years of age was asked by al-Asma'i the reason for his long life. The old man answered: 'I rejected jealousy, and that is why I have lasted so long.'

FOLK TRADITION, *Editor*

YEA, THE righteous shall keep the way of the righteous,
   and to God turn the steps of all that abideth;
And to God ye return, too; with Him, only,
   rest the issues of things – and all that they gather.

LABID, *Lyall*

A RIGHTEOUS life of hardship is better than an easy life of corruption.

AL-JAHIZ, *Editor*

PRAYER AND FASTING

RECITE WHAT is sent
Of the Book by inspiration
To thee, and establish
Regular Prayer: for Prayer
Restrains from shameful
And unjust deeds;
And remembrance of God
Is the greatest (thing in life)
Without doubt. And God knows
The (deeds) that ye do.

QUR'AN 29: 45

THERE IS a polish for everything that taketh away rust; and the polish for the heart is the remembrance of God.

HADITH

FASTING IS an armour with which one protects oneself; so let not him (who fasts) utter immodest (or foul) speech, nor let him act in an ignorant manner; and if a man quarrels with him or abuses him, he should say twice, I am fasting.

HADITH

I AM more afraid of being hindered from prayer than of being denied an answer to my prayer.

AL-JAHIZ, *Nicholson*

THE NOBLEST of these observances from a certain point of view is that one in which the performer assumes that he is addressing God in private converse, that he is turning to God and standing before Him. This observance is Prayer.

IBN SINA, *Arberry*

LIFE AND DEATH

VERILY THE knowledge
Of the Hour is
With God (alone).
It is He Who sends down
Rain, and He Who knows
What is in the wombs.
Nor does any one know
What it is that he will
Earn on the morrow:
Nor does any one know
In what land he is
To die. Verily with God
Is full knowledge and He
Is acquainted (with all things).

QUR'AN 31: 34

WE MADE from water
Every living thing.

QUR'AN 21: 30

VERILY IT is We Who
Give Life and Death;
And to Us is
The Final Goal.

QUR'AN 50: 43

THE WORLD is founded on four things – a learned man who puts his learning to good use, an ignorant man who refuses not to seek learning, a rich man who is generous in his giving, and a poor man who would never barter his after-life for a worldly-life.

'ALI IBN ABI TALEB, *Editor*

WE SPIN about and whirl our way through life,
    Then, rich and poor alike, at last seek rest
Below the ground in hollow pits slate-covered;
    And there we do abide.

ABU TAMMAM, *Hitti*

A PASSER-BY STOPPED at the door of a house in which a dead man was being mourned by his weeping relatives, and said 'How strange! These people are mourning a traveller who has finally reached his destination.'

FOLK TRADITION, Editor

THE GRAVE and Cradle, the untiring twain,
Who in the markets of this narrow lane
    Bordered of darkness, ever give and take
In equal measure – what's the loss or gain?

AL-MA'ARRI, Rihani

WHERE ARE the Kings and the peoples of the earth? They
    have quitted that which they have built and peopled;
And in the grave they are pledged for their past actions:
    there after destruction, they have become putrid corpses.
Where are the troops? They repelled not, nor profited.
    And where is that which they collected and hoarded?
The decree of the Lord of the Throne surprised them.
    Neither riches nor refuge saved them from it.

ARABIAN NIGHTS, Lane

WHO LIVES dies, and who dies flies; and all what is growing devours what is going.

QIS IBN SA'EDAH AL-AYADI, *Sprenger*

DO FOR this world what shall sustain you throughout your stay in it and for the next world do likewise.

FOLK TRADITION, *Editor*

THE FEET of a son of Adam will not stir (from the place of Judgment) until he be asked of three things – his youth, how he wore it away; his life, how he passed it; and his wealth, whence he got it and on what he spent it.

AL-JAHIZ, *Nicholson*

DEATH IS merely a move from the worldly abode to the abode of eternity; death is not the end of life.

IBN 'ARABI, *Editor*

EVERY SUMMARY has a trend
Every question has an answer
Every event has an hour
Every action has its account
Every ascent has its limit
Every man has his book of fate.

ABU AL-'ATAHIYA, *Howarth and Shukrallah*

DEATH IS no mean archer. Mark how his arrows hit.

LABID, *Blunt*

THE DAY that passes never returns
The day in which you are does not last
The day to come is unknown in what and whom it brings.

FOLK TRADITION, *Editor*

O DEATH! be thou my guest; I am tired of living,
And I have tried both sorts in joy and sorrow.
My morrow shall be my yesterday, none doubts it;
My yesterday nevermore shall be my morrow.

AL-MA'ARRI, *Nicholson*

I WELCOME Death in his onset and the return thereof,
That he may cover me with his garment's redundancy.
This world is such an abode that if those present here
Have their wits entire, they will never weep for the
    absent ones.

AL-MA'ARRI, *Nicholson*

I AM weary of life who bear its burdens fourscore and how
    many years of glory and grief counted. Well may he
    weary be,
I know to-day, the day before it, ay, and the days that
    were, yet of to-morrow I know nothing.

ZUHAYR IBN ABI SULMA, *Blunt*

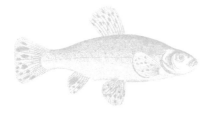

O LEVELLING Death! to thee a rich man is like a poor,
Thou car'st not that one hath hit the right way, another
    missed.
The knight's coat of mail thou deem'st in softness a
    maiden's shift,
And frail as the spider's house the domed halls of
    Chosroes.
To earth came he down unhorsed when Death in the
    saddle sate,
Tho' aye 'mongst his clan was he the noblest of them that
    ride.
A bier is but like a ship: it casteth its wrecked away
To drown in a sea of death where wave ever mounts on
    wave.

AL-MAʿARRI, *Nicholson*

FATE, RESIGNATION AND ACQUIESCENCE

TIME CONSISTS of two days; this, bright; and that, gloomy:
and life, of two moieties; this, safe; and that, fearful.

Say to him who hath taunted us on account of
misfortunes, Doth fortune oppose any but the
eminent?

Dost thou not observe that corpses float upon the sea,
while the precious pearls remain in its furthest
depths?

When the hands of time play with us, misfortune is
imparted to us by its protracted kiss.

In the heaven are stars that cannot be numbered; but
none is eclipsed save the sun and the moon.

How many green and dry trees are on the earth; but none
is assailed with stones save that which beareth fruit!

Thou thoughtest well of the days when they went well
with thee, and fearedst not the evil that destiny was
bringing.

ARABIAN NIGHTS, *Lane*

NOTHING AFFORD[S] so much tranquillity to the mind as submission to destiny.

KALILA AND DIMNA, *Knatchbull*

HE WHO trusts fate is usually betrayed.

FOLK TRADITION, *Editor*

WE TROD the steps appointed for us: and the man whose steps are appointed must tread them.
He whose death is decreed to take place in one land will not die in any land but that.

ARABIAN NIGHTS, *Lane*

THEY LOOK not on Weal as men who know not that Woe comes, too:
they look not on evil days as though they would never mend.

AL-NABIGHAH, *Lyall*

THAT HE who flieth his fate shall meet it, not, though a
    sky-ladder he should climb, shall his fear fend him:
    dark death shall noose him down.

ZUHAYR IBN ABI SULMA, *Blunt*

IF ONE were to observe the greater calamity of others, he would
    find his own calamity insignificant.

FOLK TRADITION, *Editor*

O ANGRY fate, forbear! or, if thou wilt not forbear, relent!
Neither favour from fortune do I gain, nor profit from the
    work of my hands.
I came forth to seek my sustenance, but have found it to
    be exhausted.
How many of the ignorant are in splendour! and how
    many of the wise, in obscurity!

ARABIAN NIGHTS, *Lane*

I HAVE seen the Dooms trample men as a blind beast at
    random treads:
whom they smote, he died; whom they missed, he lived
    on to strengthless eld.

ZUHAYR IBN ABI SULMA, Lyall

HOW MANY by my labors, that evermore endure, All goods
    of life enjoy and in cooly shade recline?
Each morn that dawns I wake in travail and in woe, And
    strange is my condition and my burden gars me pine:
Many others are in luck and from miseries are free, And
    Fortune never loads them with loads the like o' mine:
They live their happy days in all solace and delight; Eat,
    drink, and dwell in honor 'mid the noble and the digne:
All living things were made of a little drop of sperm,
    Thine origin is mine and my provenance is thine;
Yet the difference and distance 'twixt the twain of us are
    far, As the difference of savor 'twix vinegar and wine:
But at Thee, O God All-wise! I venture not to rail, Whose
    ordinance is just and whose justice cannot fail.

ARABIAN NIGHTS, Burton

GRATITUDE FOR BLESSINGS RECEIVED

O YE who believe!
Eat of the good things
That We have provided for you,
And be grateful to God,
If it is Him ye worship.

QUR'AN 2: 172

IF I FAIL any day to render thee due thanks, tell me for
    whom I have composed my verse and prose
Thou hast loaded me with favours unsolicited, bestowed
    without delay on thy part, or excuse.
How then should I abstain from praising thee as thou
    deservest, and lauding thee both with my heart and
    voice?
Nay, I will thank thee for thy benefits conferred upon me:
    they are light upon my tongue, though weighty to my
    back.

ARABIAN NIGHTS, *Lane*

WHEN ONE reflects upon the bounties that God has bestowed on him, and how little he is thankful for them, he becomes ashamed of asking for more because of how much he has attained thus far.

SA'IDA BINT ZAYD, *Cornell*

THE EXPRESSION of gratitude has three stations: love in the heart, praise on the tongue, and reward by action.

FOLK TRADITION, *Editor*

IF YOU are granted a blessing from God, hurry toward it with thankfulness before it disappears.

HIND BINT AL-MUHALLAB, *Cornell*

AND GUARD thee of complaining, thou hearest no man of sense complain, but the fool, who snarls and growls while he checks himself.

AL-HARIRI, *Steingass*

Gratitude for Blessings Received ❧ 51

O MY Joy and my Desire and my Refuge,
My Friend and my Sustainer and my Goal,
Thou art my Intimate, and longing for Thee sustains me,
Were it not for Thee, O my Life and my Friend,
How I should have been distraught over the spaces of the
 earth,
How many favours have been bestowed, and how much
 hast Thou given me.
Of gifts and grace and assistance,
Thy love is now my desire and my bliss,
And has been revealed to the eye of my heart that was
 athirst,
I have none beside Thee, Who dost make the desert
 blossom,
Thou art my joy, firmly established within me,
If Thou art satisfied with me, then
O Desire of my heart, my happiness has appeared.

RABI'A AL-'ADAWIYYA, *Smith*

THE FORTUNATE man is he to whom God sufficeth, and who hath
 no need of other than him.

ARABIAN NIGHTS, *Payne*

BEING VIRTUOUS

VIRTUE AND ETHICS

WHEN A (courteous) greeting
Is offered you, meet it
With a greeting still more
Courteous, or (at least)
Of equal courtesy.
God takes careful account
Of all things.

QUR'AN 4: 86

HE WHO preaches prejudice is not one of our number.

HADITH

A MAN'S conduct is a measure of his faith.

HADITH

NO ONE can be considered a believer until he desires for his
brother whatever he desires for himself.

HADITH

EVERY NATION has virtues and vices and every people has good and bad qualities, and every group of people is both complete and deficient in its industry and its wielding of influence. And it is decreed that bounties and merits and faults be poured forth over all mankind, scattered among them all.

AL-TAWHIDI, *Damis*

BACKBITE NOT, lest thou be backbitten; for probably, of
    him who saith a thing, the like will be said:
And abstain from shameful words: utter them not when
    thou speakest seriously or when thou jestest.

ARABIAN NIGHTS, *Lane*

I WISH to live free of hate;
I wish to love free of jealousy;
I wish to rise in the world free of the feeling of
    superiority;
I wish to go forward without stepping on anyone below
    me, or envying anyone above me.

AMEEN RIHANI, *Editor*

A MAN ... is distinguished from the beasts by four qualities, wisdom, temperance, understanding, and justice. Knowledge, urbanity, and considerateness, form essential parts of wisdom. Clemency, patience and firmness, belong to understanding. Modesty, nobleness, inclination, and aversion, are under the control of temperance. Sincerity, goodness, piety, and the amiable affections, are inseparable from justice; and when a person is in full possession of these bright qualities, neither the excess of good fortune is capable of betraying him into any wayward and perverse measures, which will throw him into trouble and disappointment, nor does he wantonly indulge in complaints against Providence for every slight interruption which is offered to his enjoyments. The decrees of fate do not discompose the serenity of his looks, nor a sudden reverse disturb his peace of mind; his wisdom is a treasure which cannot be diminished by expenditure, it is an imperishable store under the pressure of poverty and want, it is a robe, which does not lose by use the appearance of being new, and whose intrinsic worth remains always unimpaired, and it becomes a pleasure of unlimited duration.

KALILA AND DIMNA, *Knatchbull*

THE BEST of all attributes is courtesy.

FOLK TRADITION, *Editor*

BE DIGNIFIED in adversity,
Patient in calamity,
Thankful in prosperity,
Humble in prayer,
Swift in offering charity.

FOLK TRADITION, *Editor*

THE WAY of vice is open as the sky,
The way of virtue's like the needle's eye;
    But whether here or there, the eager Soul
Has only two Companions, – Whence and Why.

AL-MA'ARRI, *Rihani*

A MAN of refinement avoids three things when in the company of others: trivial jesting because it breeds hatred, talk of women because it demonstrates a diminished sense of honour, and elaborate mention of food because it suggests that he is a glutton.

FOLK TRADITION, *Editor*

THREE QUALITIES cannot be recognized except in three
   types of men:
The magnanimous man can only be recognized when
   provoked by anger,
The brave man can only be recognized when in the thick
   of the battle,
And the true brother can only be recognized when you
   are in dire need of him.

FOLK TRADITION, *Editor*

WHAT! SEEST thou not that vice in man's nature is inborn,
But virtue a new unheired possession which minds
   acquire?

AL-MA'ARRI, *Nicholson*

REMEMBER THAT courage is the foundation of all virtues. He
who is devoid of courage will not be able to honour any of
the virtues through perseverance and inner strength.

FOLK TRADITION, *Editor*

GOODNESS AND INNOCUITY

GOOD IS (the reward)
For those who do good
In this world.
Spacious is God's earth!
Those who patiently persevere
Will truly receive
A reward without measure!

QUR'AN 39: 10

MUHAMMAD SAID, 'O Wábísah! are you come to ask what is goodness and what is badness?' Wábísah said, 'Yes, I am come for that.' Then he joined his fingers and struck them upon Wábísah's breast, that is, made a sign towards his heart, and said, 'Ask the question from thine own heart.' This he repeated three times and said, 'Goodness is a thing from which thy heart findeth firmness and rest; and badness is a thing which throweth thee into doubt, although men may acquit thee.'

HADITH

THE MOST meritorious of good deeds is that which is done quickly.

FOLK TRADITION, Editor

THE ESSENCE of all goodness is found in a steadfast heart.

FOLK TRADITION, Editor

SOW GOOD, even on an unworthy soil; for it will not be
fruitless wherever it is sown.
Verily, good, though it remain long buried, none will reap
but he who sowed it.

ARABIAN NIGHTS, Lane

HE WHO does not know what evil is deserves to fall on it.

'UMAR IBN AL-KHATTAB, Editor

FROM THORNS you cannot harvest grapes.

FOLK TRADITION, Editor

WHEN GOD'S aid promoteth the business of a man, his
  wish, in every case, is easily accomplished:
But if the aid of God be not granted to a man, the first
  thing that harmeth him is his own endeavour.

ARABIAN NIGHTS, Lane

BLESSED IS he who is so busy in dealing with his own faults that he
  has no time to observe the faults of others.

FOLK TRADITION, Editor

A MAN is known among others by his actions, and the deeds
  of the ingenuous and generous are like his origin ...
In the sky is written, upon the pages of the air, He who
  doth kind actions will experience the like.

ARABIAN NIGHTS, Lane

HE THAT shows the way to goodness is equal to him that practises
  it.

FOLK TRADITION, Levy

DAVID WANTED to construct the Temple, and he did so several times, but whenever he finished it, it fell down. Then, David complained of that to God. God revealed to him, 'My temple shall not be built by the hand of one who shed blood.' When David said, 'Oh, Lord wasn't that done for Your sake?' He answered, 'Yes, but they were also My servants.'

IBN 'ARABI, *Takeshita*

FORSAKE EVIL and evil shall forsake you, for evil hastens unto those who work evil.

FOLK TRADITION, *Editor*

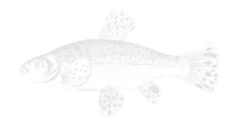

HONESTY AND HYPOCRISY

FALSEHOOD ... is a bar to all intimacy and fellowship.

KALILA AND DIMNA, *Knatchbull*

AN IGNORANT man who is true is better than a clever man who is false.

FOLK TRADITION, *Wortabet*

FROM HIS tongue nothing but words of sweetness come,
While like a fox in treacherous craftiness his work is done.

FOLK TRADITION, *Editor*

DECEIT [IS] one of the worst crimes which a man can commit, and ... treachery and cunning never lead to good; ... he who practises them, is always the victim of his own contrivances, and the author of wrong severely atones for the propensity which he has encouraged.

KALILA AND DIMNA, *Knatchbull*

STRAIGHTEN YOURSELF and people will be straight with you.

FOLK TRADITION, *Editor*

'THE WINE'S forbidden,' say these honest folk,
But for themselves the law they will revoke;
   The snivelling sheikh says he's without a garb
When in the tap-house he had pawned his cloak.

AL-MA'ARRI, *Rihani*

OPEN BLAME is better than secret malice.

FOLK TRADITION, *Wortabet*

REVILE NOT the Devil publicly while you secretly cherish his
friendship.

WAHB IBN MUNABIH, *Editor*

BETWEEN YOU and that which is unlawful erect a barrier of what is
lawful.

FOLK TRADITION, *Editor*

WHEN MY wealth faileth, no friend assisteth me; but when it aboundeth, all men are my friends.
How many enemies for the sake of wealth have consorted with me! And my companion, in the time of want, hath abandoned me!

ARABIAN NIGHTS, Lane

JEALOUSY, LIES and hypocrisy are the vilest forms of debasement.

FOLK TRADITION, Editor

THE MOST miserable of men is he who desires a station far above his own.

FOLK TRADITION, Editor

DELIVER ME from him who does not tell the truth unless he stings; and from the man of good conduct and bad intentions; and from him who acquires self-esteem by finding fault in others.

KAHLIL GIBRAN, Ferris

YOUR FRIEND is he who tells you the truth, not he who agrees with everything you say.

FOLK TRADITION, *Sabbagh*

HEARTS ARE the depositories of secrets, lips their locks, and tongues their keys.

FOLK TRADITION, *Wortabet*

IF A man performs a good deed and refrains from declaring it, and then wishes people to know what good he has done, such a man is counted among the vilest of hypocrites.

FOLK TRADITION, *Editor*

MERCY, SYMPATHY AND COMPASSION

B E RECONCILED with the one who has severed the ties of friendship with you, forgive him who is unjust towards you, and be generous towards him who has denied you his favours.

HADITH

IF YOU cannot help men with money, help them with a cheerful face and a kindly bearing.

FOLK TRADITION, Wortabet

HE WHO speaks the kind word should be loved.

'ALI IBN ABI TALEB, Editor

WHEN FORTUNE is liberal to thee, be thou liberal to all others before she escape from thee:
For liberality will not annihilate thy wealth when she is favourable; nor avarice preserve it when she deserteth thee.

ARABIAN NIGHTS, Lane

QUENCH BY thy mercy the fire of anger that recklessly a
   churl has kindled in thee, and pardon his trespass,
For mercy is far the best of jewels that grace the wise,
   and sweetest fruit, culled by man, is ready forgiveness.

AL-HARIRI, Steingass

DOST THOU not see that what thou lovest and what thou
   hatest are conjoined?
And that the delight of long life is disturbed by the
   mixture of grey hairs?
And that the thorns appear upon the branches together
   with the fruit that is gathered?
Who is he that hath never done evil? And who hath done
   good alone?
If thou triedst the sons of this age, thou wouldst find that
   most of them had erred.

ARABIAN NIGHTS, Lane

TRUTH

THE TRUTH (comes)
From God alone;
So be not of those
Who doubt.

QUR'AN 3: 60

NO MAN is true in the truest sense of the word but he who is true
in word, in deed, and in thought.

HADITH

AH, THE black swarm of the poets have emptied
   reproaches upon me –
What is incurably rotten is not adapted for praise.
Lips that have drunk of the foulness of putrified waters
Cry that the heart of a crystalline torrent is foul.

AL-MUTANABBI, *Baerlein*

BY FEARING whom I trust I find my way
To truth; by trusting wholly I betray
    The trust of wisdom; better far is doubt,
Which brings the false into the light of day.

AL-MA'ARRI, Rihani

WE SEEK a religion the essence of which is the knowledge of God and ignorance of theology. We seek a religion that teaches people everywhere the brotherhood of man.

AMEEN RIHANI, Editor

KEEP TO truth, although it scorch thee with the fire of threatening:
And seek to please God; for the most foolish of mankind is he who angers the master and pleases the slave.

AL-HARIRI, Chenery

THE DOUBTS of the wise are more valid than the certainty of the foolish.

FOLK TRADITION, Editor

MANY A door opens the way to God.

FOLK TRADITION, *Editor*

HE SAW the lightning in the east and he longed for the east,
but if it had flashed in the west he would have longed
for the west.
My desire is for the lightning and its gleam, not for the
places and the earth.

IBN 'ARABI, *Nicholson*

YOU SING about the smallness of the stars –
The fault is in your eye, not in the stars.

AL-MA'ARRI, *Baerlein*

IN ALL the religions of the world there is a light that shines for a
while and will not be extinguished until another light shines
in its place.

AMEEN RIHANI, *Editor*

SO TOO the creeds of Man: the one prevails
Until the other comes; and this one fails
   When that one triumphs; ay, the lonesome world
Will always want the latest fairy-tales.

AL-MA'ARRI, Rihani

IT BEHOVES us never to shy away from showing approbation of the truth wherever it comes from, be it from faraway races or from strange and different nations. For nothing is more worthy of him who seeks the truth than to recognise it [whatever its source]. It also behoves us never to degrade the truth, nor to disparage him who speaks it or him who conveys it. For no man is degraded by the truth; all are honoured and elevated by it.

AL-KINDI, Editor

MOHAMMAD OR Messiah! Hear thou me,
The truth entire nor here nor there can be;
   How can our God who made the sun and moon
Give all his light to one Sect, I can not see.

AL-MA'ARRI, Rihani

THE TRUTH that needs proof is only half true.

KAHLIL GIBRAN, *Ferris*

'WHAT IS thy faith and creed,' they ask of me,
'And who art thou? Unseal thy pedigree.' –
    I am the child of Time, my tribe, mankind,
And now this world's my caravanseri.

AL-MA'ARRI, *Rihani*

I NEVER doubted a truth that needed an explanation unless I
    found myself having to analyse the explanation.

KAHLIL GIBRAN, *Ferris*

NOW, MOSQUES and churches – even a Kaaba Stone,
Korans and Bibles – even a martyr's bone, –
    All these and more my heart can tolerate,
For my religion's love, and love alone.

AL-MA'ARRI, *Rihani*

JUSTICE

GOD COMMANDS justice, the doing
Of good, and liberality to kith
And kin, and He forbids
All shameful deeds, and injustice
And rebellion: He instructs you,
That ye may receive admonition.

QUR'AN 16: 90

FOR THE white to domineer over the black, the Arab over the non-Arab, the rich over the poor, the strong over the weak or men over women is both wrong and unseemly.

HADITH

HE WHO unsheathes his sword of aggression is bound to suffer its sharp edge.

HADITH

THE WORST of men is he who champions the oppressor and
   abandons the oppressed.

WITH THE same judgment a person judges others, he will certainly
   be judged.

FOLK TRADITION, *Editor*

OPPRESS NOT if thou hast the power to do so; for
   oppression will eventually bring thee repentance:
Thine eye will sleep while the oppressed, wakeful, will
   call for vengeance upon thee; and the eye of God
   sleepeth not.

ARABIAN NIGHTS, *Lane*

I HAVE never feared anyone more than the man whom I have
   unjustly treated, knowing that he has none other than God to
   help him, and whose only supplication is: 'Sufficient unto me
is God; may He be the judge between us.'

FOLK TRADITION, *Editor*

JUSTICE IS the foundation of all sovereignty and dominion.

FOLK TRADITION, *Editor*

INJUSTICE BREEDS disunity.

FOLK TRADITION, *Editor*

JUSTICE UNIFIES all hearts.

FOLK TRADITION, *Editor*

FIDELITY, LOYALTY AND
RESPONSIBILITY TO OBLIGATION

THE FAITHFUL in their mutual compassion, sympathy and love are exemplified by the whole body. If one of its organs falls ill, the remainder will suffer.

HADITH

AMONG THE laudable instincts, noble characteristics and virtuous habits by which men may be adorned, whether they are engaged in love-making or any other activity, Fidelity ranks high. It is one of the strongest proofs and clearest demonstrations of sound stock and pure breed; it differs in degree of excellence according to that variability which is inherent in all created beings.

IBN HAZM, *Arberry*

INJUSTICE, DECEPTION, betrayal of trust: these three, if found in a man, would destroy him.

ABU BAKR AL-SIDDIQ, *Editor*

THAT HE who guardeth not his tent-floor, with the whole
    might of him,
cold shall be his hearth-stone broken, ay, though he
    smote at none.

ZUHAYR IBN ABI SULMA, *Blunt*

TO HIDE a secret guarded well
Is no great merit, truth to tell,
But rather to conceal a thing
Which other men are whispering.

IBN HAZM, *Arberry*

DO NOT postpone today's work until the morrow.

'UMAR IBN AL-KHATTAB, *Editor*

TO BE in debt causes great worry by night and humiliation by
day. Debt is but a chain God has willed to exist on earth; if
He wishes to humiliate any of His servants, He encircles
his neck with it.

FOLK TRADITION, *Editor*

A FREEMAN'S word is his bond.

FOLK TRADITION, *Editor*

> THY FIERCEST foe is one thou dost not fight:
> Thy kindest friend is one far out of sight.
> Much knowledge have I gained of men and days,
> Experiment has trained me in their ways.
> And from the furthest furthest is my fear;
> While danger from the nearest is most near.
> The trusted comrade is the foe who harms:
> The enemy avowéd least alarms.
> That is no home where none has friendly mind:
> They are no kinfolk of whom none is kind.
> Connexion is connexion of the heart;
> Thy neighbour he who distant takes thy part.

ABU FIRAS AL-HAMADHANI, *Margoliouth*

THOSE NEAREST to you are the ones most worthy of your favours.

FOLK TRADITION, *Editor*

K NOW THAT the contract of brotherhood is a bond between two persons, like the contract of marriage between two spouses. For just as marriage gives rise to certain duties which must be fulfilled when it is entered into, so does the contract of brotherhood confer upon your brother a certain right touching your property, your person, your tongue and your heart – by way of forgiveness, prayer, sincerity, loyalty, relief and considerateness.

AL-GHAZZALI, *Holland*

T HE FIRST degree of fidelity is for a man to be faithful to one who is faithful to him. This indeed is an absolute duty, an obligation binding upon lover and beloved alike: no man deviates from it, unless he be of mean extraction and devoid of every grace and virtue.

IBN HAZM, *Arberry*

THE ART OF
SELF-RESTRAINT

فَٱسْتَقِمْ كَمَآ أُمِرْتَ

RESOLUTION, EFFORT AND ENDEAVOUR

GO ABROAD from the home-lands in search of eminence,
    and travel, for in travel are five advantages:
The dissipation of anxiety, the acquisition of a livelihood,
    knowledge, culture, and the society of some noble one.
And if it be said, 'In travels are humiliation and trouble,
    the traversing of deserts and the encountering of
    hardships,'
Yet the death of a brave man is better for him than his
    continuance in the mansion of abasement, between
    humiliation and an envious rival.

FOLK TRADITION, *Browne*

STRIVE ALWAYS for the highest, you will gain the highest
    seat,
And have the half-moon's silver for the covering of your
    feet.

AL-MUTANABBI, *Baerlein*

MOVEMENT IS a great blessing.

FOLK TRADITION, *Editor*

THE BEST gift of God to man is understanding... Understanding is the child of instruction and experience; its seeds lie hidden in the soul of man, and must be called into life by the nurturing hand of discipline and fortified by trial, as the sparks are struck out from the hard flint, before the fire, which lies concealed in the stone, can be produced.

KALILA AND DIMNA, *Knatchbull*

BY MEANS of toil man shall scale the height;
Who to fame aspires mustn't sleep o' night:
Who seeketh pearl in the deep must dive,
Winning weal and wealth by his main and might:
And who seeketh Fame without toil and strife
Th' impossible seeketh and wasteth life.

ARABIAN NIGHTS, *Burton*

JOURNEYS ARE a trial.

FOLK TRADITION, *Levy*

A MAN of sense, when a weighty matter seems pregnant with mischief to himself and those with whom he is connected, will submit without reluctance to the severest trials of his patience, when he has the prospect of a happy issue to his endurance and resignation; he neither repines at the pains which he is obliged to undergo, nor at the mortifying humiliation of a temporary compliance with the will of an inferior, looking to the attainment of the object which he has in view as a sufficient recompence for all his toils and sufferings.

KALILA AND DIMNA, *Knatchbull*

THE RESOLUTIONS a man makes are a measure of his resolve;
   The gifts a man makes are a measure of his
    munificence.
Small acts loom large in the eyes of small men;
   And mighty deeds seem as nothing in the eyes of the
   great!

AL-MUTANABBI, *Editor*

IF FAME thou seekest, wed thyself to toil,
Divorce thy consciousness from earth's turmoil;
  To rob a honeycomb is hard indeed;
A sting thou mayest expect before the spoil.

AL-MUTANABBI, Beder

I T IS not however fit, that a man should ... neglect the
necessary means for the improvement of his temporal
condition, or that he should rely on a fortuitous and happy
combination of circumstances to deliver him out of all his
difficulties and trouble; for an extraordinary interposition of fate
very seldom occurs; and mankind in general are doomed to owe
their advancement and success in life to their own exertions, and
to the means which it is in the power of every one to make use of,
which however should be applied to the acquisition of some solid
and permanent good; for whoever fixes his thoughts on an
inappropriate object, where his solicitude and anxious attention
can only end in disappointment and trouble, is like the dove,
who having hatched and lost her young ones, did not take
warning, but made her nest in the same place, and was in this
manner robbed of her second brood.

KALILA AND DIMNA, Knatchbull

Resolution, Effort and Endeavour ❧ 85

FORGIVENESS, MAGNANIMITY
AND SELF-CONTROL

BUT INDEED if any
Show patience and forgive,
That would truly be
An exercise of courageous will
And resolution in the conduct
Of affairs

QUR'AN 42: 43

VERILY THE most beloved of you by me, and nearest to me in the next world, are those of good dispositions; and verily the greatest enemies to me and the farthest from me, are the ill-tempered.

HADITH

'GIVE ME advice,' said someone. Muhammad said, 'Be not angry.'

HADITH

OF ALL the enemies I have known, I found none more inveterate than raging anger.

FOLK TRADITION, *Editor*

SUPPOSE I have committed a crime: forgive it. For, by Allah, how sweet is the beloved when he pardoneth!

ARABIAN NIGHTS, *Lane*

CONTENTED EYES to all the faults are blind;
but eyes displeased will only weakness find.

FOLK TRADITION, *Sabbagh*

KNOW YE not that the most precious of offerings is the relieving of sorrows, and the firmest cord of salvation is the imparting to those who have need?

AL-HARIRI, *Chenery*

IN BEING magnanimous towards an impudent man, you will increase the number of those who will champion you against him.

FOLK TRADITION, Editor

> IF YOU are inclined to reproach your friend over every matter, you will not find anyone whom you never have cause to reproach.
> So live in solitude, or be in amity with your brother; sometimes he may avoid a fault, but sometimes cling to it.
> If you do not at times drink a bitter cup and endure it, you must go thirsty; what man is there whose drink is always limpid?

BASHSHAR, Bakalla

> BEWARE OF losing hearts in consequence of injury, for the bringing them back, after flight, is difficult.
> Verily hearts, when affection hath fled from them, are like glass, which, when broken, cannot be made whole again.

ARABIAN NIGHTS, Lane

PARDON THY brother when he mingles his right aiming
   with error;
And shrink from rebuking him if he swerve or decline;
Keep faith with him even though he fail in what thou and
   he have stipulated;
And know that if thou seek a perfect man thou desirest
   beyond bounds.
Who is there who has never done ill? Who is there whose
   deed is always fair?
Dost thou not see the loved and the hated linked together
   in one class,
As the thorn comes forth on the branches with the fruit
   that is gathered.
And the delight of long life, lo! there mingles with it the
   trouble of hoariness.
If thou examine well the sons of the time thou wilt find
   the most of them but refuse.

AL-HARIRI, *Chenery*

I WILL restrain my heart from opposing [your] enemies,
   for what I have met of tears suffices me.

DIBIL, *Zolondek*

THE ARABS say there is no triumphant glory in taking revenge, for the wise man, if Almighty God should assist him, would never allow anger to be one of his traits.

FOLK TRADITION, Editor

O SOUL, do not despair over the gravity of your faults;
Great sins when forgiveness comes are like small ones.

AL-BUSIRI, Sperl and Shackle

IF YOU are able to overcome your enemy, forgive him as a token of your gratitude that you possess the power to do so.

'ALI IBN ABI TALEB, Editor

KINDNESS SUBDUES the man of generous race,
But only makes more insolent the base.
As ill doth bounty in sword's place accord
With honour as in bounty's place the sword.

AL-MUTANABBI, Nicholson

DETACHMENT

O YE who believe! what
Is the matter with you,
That, when ye are asked
To go forth in the Cause of God,
Ye cling heavily to the earth?
Do ye prefer the life
Of this world to the Hereafter?
But little is the comfort
Of this life, as compared
With the Hereafter.

QUR'AN 9: 38

DESIRE NOT the world, and God will love you; and desire not what
men have, and they will love you.

HADITH

MAN ALWAYS desires that which is forbidden.

FOLK TRADITION, *Editor*

❧ 92 ❧

IF [ONE] does not cling with his affections to artificial wants, he can bear their loss without a sigh.

KALILA AND DIMNA, *Knatchbull*

A WISE man was asked: 'Do you know what is greater than gold?' He answered: 'He who renounces gold.'

FOLK TRADITION, *Editor*

SOME SAY that the Devil exhibits the world to the people every day, asking 'Who will buy a ware that will do him harm and no good, and bring him care and no delight?' Those who frequent the world and adore it reply 'We will.' He tells them 'Its price is not pence or pounds but your share in paradise. I purchased it with four things: the curse, the wrath, the fury, and the persecution of God. And I sold paradise for it.' They say 'We accept the same.' He tells them 'I am trying to rook you.' They answer 'So be it.' Whereupon he sells them the world, commenting 'A bad bargain.'

AL-GHAZZALI, *Howarth and Shukrallah*

AVARICE … is not excused by the multitude of its possessions.

KALILA AND DIMNA, Knatchbull

THERE ARE three kinds of slaves: a slave in bondage, a slave of lust, and a slave of greed.

FOLK TRADITION, Editor

WHATEVER IS past and has come to an end cannot be brought back by sorrow.

IBN ZUHR, Arberry

SILENCE AND SOLITUDE

MUCH SILENCE and a good disposition, there are no two works better than those.

HADITH

MANY A word says to its speaker: 'Let me be.'

FOLK TRADITION, *Editor*

THE TONGUE is a lion which must be chained, and a sharp sword which must be sheathed.

FOLK TRADITION, *Wortabet*

IT IS better to remain silent than to argue with those who are ignorant.

AL-JAHIZ, *Editor*

A SLIP of the foot is safer than a slip of the tongue. A false step may break a bone which can be set, but a slip of the tongue cannot be undone.

FOLK TRADITION, *Wortabet*

SILENCE IS wisdom.

FOLK TRADITION, *Editor*

N OT EVERY thing that a man knows can be revealed, nor can everything that he can reveal be considered as timely, nor can every timely utterance be considered suitable to the capacity of those who hear it.

FOLK TRADITION, *Editor*

IF SPEECH is silver, silence is gold.

FOLK TRADITION, *Editor*

PATIENCE

AND OBEY God and His Apostle;
And fall into no disputes,
Lest ye lose heart
And your power depart;
And be patient and persevering:
For God is with those
Who patiently persevere.

QUR'AN 8: 46

HE WHO carefully considers the consequences of his actions
before he acts avoids disaster.

FOLK TRADITION, *Editor*

WHAT FORTUNE bringeth thee affliction, console thyself by
remembering that one day thou must see prosperity,
and another day, difficulty.

ARABIAN NIGHTS, *Lane*

PATIENCE HAS three stages: first, it means that the servant ceases to complain, and this is the stage of repentance: second, he becomes satisfied with what is decreed, and this is the rank of the ascetics: third, he comes to love whatever his Lord does with him and this is the stage of the true friends of God.

ABU TALIB AL-MAKKI, *Smith*

HASTE IS the sister of regret.

FOLK TRADITION, *Editor*

BE MILD when thou art troubled by rage, and be patient when calamity befalleth thee;
For the nights are pregnant with events, and give birth to every kind of wonder.

ARABIAN NIGHTS, *Lane*

CONSIDER THE doings of thy Lord, how happiness cometh unto thee, with speedy relief;
And despair not when thou sufferest affliction; for how many wondrous mercies attend affliction!

ARABIAN NIGHTS, *Lane*

THE KEY to success is patience.

FOLK TRADITION, *Editor*

GOD TRIES him whom He loves.

FOLK TRADITION, *Editor*

BE PATIENT: for freeborn men to bear is the fairest thing,
And refuge against Time's wrong or help from his hurt is
    none;
And if it availed man aught to bow him to fluttering Fear,
Or if he could ward off hurt by humbling himself to Ill,
To bear with a valiant front the full brunt of every stroke
And onset of Fate were still the fairest and best of things.
But how much the more, when none outruns by a span
    his Doom,
And refuge from God's decree nor was nor will ever be,
And sooth, if the changing Days have wrought us – their
    wonted way –
A lot mixed of weal and woe, yet one thing they could not
    do:
They have not made soft or weak the stock of our sturdy
    spear;

They have not abased our hearts to doing of deeds of
    shame.
We offer to bear their weight, a handful of noble souls:
Though laden beyond all weight of man, they uplift the
    load.
So shield we with Patience fair our souls from the stroke
    of Shame;
Our honors are whole and sound, though others be lean
    enow.

IBRAHIM IBN KUNAIF, *Lyall*

HE WHO is endowed with patience eventually triumphs.

FOLK TRADITION, *Editor*

I WILL endure with patience, O my Lord, what Thou hast
    ordered. I will be patient, if so I may obtain thine
    approval.
They have tyrannized over us, and transgressed, and
    commanded. Perhaps, in thy beneficence, Thou wilt
    pardon what is past.

ARABIAN NIGHTS, *Lane*

OBEDIENCE

O YE who believe!
Obey God, and obey the Apostle,
And those charged
With authority among you.
If ye differ in anything
Among yourselves, refer it
To God and His Apostle,
If ye do believe in God
And the Last Day:
That is best, and most suitable
For final determination.

QUR'AN 4: 59

THE FAITHFUL treasurer who pays what he is ordered with a willing
heart is one of those who give charity.

HADITH

IF YOU wish to be obeyed, ask what is possible.

FOLK TRADITION, *Editor*

THE WORD of God alone is unchangeable ... whose decrees are immutable and fixed.

KALILA AND DIMNA, *Knatchbull*

A HMAD IBN Abí al-Hawárí said that he asked Umm Hárún: 'Do you desire death?' 'No,' she said. 'Why?' I asked. She replied: 'If I disobeyed a human being, I would not want to encounter him. So how could I desire to encounter God when I have disobeyed Him?'

UMM HARUN, *Cornell*

THE WISEST of men is one who obeys those who are wiser than he.

FOLK TRADITION, *Editor*

CHASTITY, MODESTY AND PURE LIFE

FOR GOD loves those
Who turn to Him constantly
And He loves those
Who keep themselves pure and clean.

QUR'AN 2: 222

TRUE MODESTY is the source of all virtues.

HADITH

OBSCENE CONVERSATION . . . is a folly in words.

KALILA AND DIMNA, *Knatchbull*

MADNESS TAKES various forms, and drunkenness is one of the
forms of madness.

FOLK TRADITION, *Levy*

WINE LEADETH astray from the path of rectitude, and openeth the doors to evil.

ARABIAN NIGHTS, *Lane*

CHASTITY IS the best form of worship.

ABU JA'FAR AL-MANSUR, *Editor*

TO ABANDON sin is better than to strive after repentance. Many a time hath one glance sown the seed of a lust, and the lust of a moment hath left a long grief behind.

AL-JAHIZ, *Nicholson*

TWO CLASSES of men are proper objects of aversion: those who deny the distinction between virtue and vice, dispute the certainty of rewards and punishments, and contest the force of obligations they have contracted; and those who never turn away their eyes from what is forbidden to look on, nor their ears from listening to what is evil, who neither check their passion for adulterous connections, nor control the heart in its inordinate and vicious propensities.

KALILA AND DIMNA, *Knatchbull*

Chastity, Modesty and Pure Life ↝ 105

AND BATTLE against lust that destroys thee, for many who had soared to the stars, enslaved by lust, fell and came to grief.

AL-HARIRI, *Steingass*

A MAN'S standing is commensurate with his prosperity; his truthfulness with his virtues; his courage with his dignity; and his chastity with his sense of honour.

'ALI IBN ABI TALEB, *Editor*

MANY ARE those who know and do not benefit; many are those who are obstinate and incline to their passions and doubts.

DIBIL, *Zolondek*

RID THE heart of thoughtlessness and the soul of lustful desires. Subdue licentiousness by the thought of the onrushing death. Fear the day when your sins will be recognized by their scars.

IBN NUBATA, *Bukhsh and Margoliouth*

I WOULD not, when she would submit,
Let Satan's prompting be obeyed.

Her face, uncovered, lit the night
    That raised its veil of shade.

But God's command forbidding lust
Stood like a chamberlain to trust,
    Guarding the gates of passion;
My instinct still must be repressed,
    Rebelling in this fashion.

So beside her now I lie
    All night and long for rest –
A camel's thirsty colt whose muzzle
    Keeps him from the breast;
Or in a garden where the eye
    Alone devours –
I'm no abandoned beast to guzzle,
    Pasturing on flowers.

IBN FARAJ, *Morland*

HUMILITY

NOR WALK on the earth
With insolence: for thou
Canst not rend the earth
Asunder, nor reach
The mountains in height.

QUR'AN 17: 37

VERILY GOD instructs me to be humble and lowly and not proud; and that no one should oppress another.

HADITH

THE BASE-NATURED is always boastful, while the noble in character is always humble.

FOLK TRADITION, *Editor*

HUMILITY IS the crown of nobility, a ladder to honour, and a means of procuring love and esteem.

FOLK TRADITION, *Wortabet*

HE WHO indulges in self-praise is a liar.

FOLK TRADITION, *Editor*

AND THE carcasses of the desert float upon the sea, while the fine pearl lies neglected on its lowest sands.

ARABIAN NIGHTS, *Lane*

BE HUMBLE and like a star reflected on the face of water below, yet far above all in the sky.
And do not be like the smoke that allows itself to rise above the clouds, yet will always be of the lowest dust.

FOLK TRADITION, *Editor*

THE WORST of men is he who regards himself above all other men.

'ALI IBN ABI TALEB, *Editor*

Humility ❧ 109

A WISE man was once asked whether he knew of any good which is not coveted, or any evil which deserves no mercy, and he said: 'Yes, they are humility and pride.'

FOLK TRADITION, *Wortabet*

L EARN TO say 'I do not know', because when you say I do not know others will teach you until you know. But if you were to say 'I know', others will ask you questions until you will not know.

FOLK TRADITION, *Editor*

HIDE THE good you do, and make known the good done to you.

'ALI IBN ABI TALEB, *Anonymous*

THE SERVILE is touched by humiliation in the same way that a corpse is affected by pain.

FOLK TRADITION, *Editor*

DAILY LIFE

NATURE

IS IT not in the winds our love reposes,
Which are ambassadors of all the roses?
Is not the lord of rocks and trees their lover
And of the flowers that strive his land to cover?
But man is earth's uncomfortable guest
Until she takes him on her lap, to rest.

AL-MA'ARRI, *Baerlein*

HAIL, JASMINE flower, on thy liquid stem,
Among the mountain peaks, delighting them,
Pure as the mountains that arrayed
Are in green sandals and green, silky shade.

What seest thou, what passing flight
Of dream is in thy sight?
We can but see that emerald eye
And how the pearls around it lie.

IBN DERRADSH, *Baerlein*

EARTH HAS no fairer sight to show than this its
blossom-time, With all the gently running streams
    that wander o'er its face,
It is indeed the handiwork of God Omnipotent, The
Lord of every noble gift, and Giver of all grace!

ARABIAN NIGHTS, *Payne*

CHEERFUL SPRING, laughing and swaying, has come.
His beauty almost talks. Last night Nayruz
Tiptoed through the dark and stirred sleeping buds.
A touch of dew frees petals to utter words
They could not say before. Spring dresses the trees
In a country smock embroidered with flowers.
He blesses our eyes with colours we thought forbidden.
The garden breeze is so gentle you imagine
It carries the breath of contented lovers.

AL-BUHTURI, *al-Udhari and Wightman*

NOW GARDENS underneath a tender rain
Of spring assume the robe of stripes again.

AL-BUHTURI, *Baerlein*

O COMPANION, look well around thee!
　　See how the world is decked out in spring array!
See how the white blossoms covering the hills
　　Lend to the sunny day the grace of a moonlit night!
The world has become a mere means of subsistence;
　　Then spring arrived, and lo, a beauteous spectacle
　　was unfurled!

ABU TAMMAM, *Editor*

THE BLOSSOMS are a necklace, and the branches are a neck,
the winding of the valley a forearm, and the stream a
　　bracelet.
In a garden whose shade resembled a darkness of lips,
and blossoms appeared as fine white teeth.
The branch danced in it, having drunk the moist earth,
and the doves sang, and the torrent clapped its hands.
Verdant, the moist leaves having put a robe on its body
and blossoms having assembled at its sides,
so that wherever one glanced,
a face and a downy beard appeared on every branch.

IBN KHAFAJAH, *al-Nowaihi*

THE BLISSFUL hands of spring remain
Imprisoned by their lily chain,
Young silver leaves the fortress hold
And flowers wave a sword of gold.

IBN DERRADSH, Baerlein

THERE RAINDROPS trickle through the warm, still air,
   The cloud-born firstlings of the summer skies;
Full oft I stroll in early morning there,
When, like a pearl upon a bosom fair,
   The glistening dewdrop on the sapling lies.

There the young flowerets with sweet perfume blow;
   There feathery palms their pendant clusters hold,
Like foxes' brushes waving to and fro;
There every evening comes the after-glow,
   Tipping the leaflets with its liquid gold.

BAHA'EDDIN ZUHAYR, Palmer

THE SABLE wings of Night pursuing day
Across the opalescent hills, display
    The wondrous star-gems which the fiery suns
Are scattering upon their fiery way.

AL-MA'ARRI, *Rihani*

EVERYTHING IN creation exists within you, and everything in you exists in creation. You are in borderless touch with the closest things, and, what is more, distance is not sufficient to separate you from things far away. All things, from the lowest to the loftiest, from the smallest to the greatest, exist within you as equal things. In one atom are found all the elements of the earth. One drop of water contains all the secrets of the oceans. In one motion of the mind are found all the motions of all the laws of existence.

KAHLIL GIBRAN, *Ferris*

ENJOYMENT OF THE WORLD

AT LAST the tavern-keeper heard our cries,
He came with sleep-intoxicated eyes.
Then round and round, like stars, the cups of wine he
  sent –
Like stars which clamber round the firmament.
There lay the south apparelled in a pall
Of cloud, wherefrom a fringe of showers fall;
The dusky-coloured garment had been lit
By using rainbows for the seams of it.

SEIF AL-DAWLA, *Baerlein*

FOUR THINGS banish grief and care,
Four sweet things incline
Body and soul and eyne
To enjoy, if they be there:
Water, wine,
Gardens bright and faces fair.

ABU NUWAS, *Nicholson*

O ALLAH, make my pleasures mellow
With Abû-Hafs my table-fellow!
The best enjoyment that one knows
From rosy lips and liquor flows,
From perfumed houris' amorous play,
Whenas they lilt the roundelay.

THE ABBASIDE CALIPH AL-MAHDI THE THIRD, *Lane-Poole*

MUSIC DOES not give rise, in the heart, to anything which is not already there: so he whose inner self is attached to anything else than God is stirred by music to sensual desire, but the one who is inwardly attached to the love of God is moved, by hearing music, to do His will. . .

The common folk listen to music according to nature, and the novices listen with desire and awe, while the listening of the saints brings them a vision of the Divine gifts and graces, and these are the gnostics to whom listening means contemplation. But finally, there is the listening of the spiritually perfect, to whom, through music, God reveals Himself unveiled.

SHIHAB AL-DIN ABU HAFS AL-SUHRAWARDI, *Smith*

THE STOMACH is the key to the heart.

FOLK TRADITION, *Editor*

I RUN to the wine-cup at morning, I take the same journey
    o'nights:
On my life, I can see no harm in a deed which my soul
    delights;
And one whom mine eyes confound with the moon, as
    she shines at the full –
Who is human, indeed, but of humankind the most
    beautiful –
Tendered me wine from the hand and wine from the
    honeyed lips,
And made me alone twice drunk in a circle of rips.
My comrades are all asleep ere my eyelids begin to sink,
Yet I am the first of them all to run for my morning drink.

ANONYMOUS, *Lane-Poole*

O NIGHT, whose sweets I'll ne'er forget:
All joys therein together met.
The bottle, she, and I, sat up,
And each to other passed the cup.
Did the black clusters on her head
Give wine to make her lips so red?

ABU FIRAS, *Margoliouth*

WELCOME! AND heartily, lute and reed,
    And a quaffing of wine from the hands of the slim!
The Fast is over at last, and the 'Id
    Is announced by the young moon's sickle rim;
The Pleiades fly from her greedy gape,
Which yawns like a glutton's on clustering grape.

AL-MO'TAZZ, *Lane-Poole*

MONEY AND children are the adornment of life on earth.

FOLK TRADITION, *Sabbagh*

THE ARABS

ARAB IDENTITY is in the tongue; whoever speaks Arabic is an Arab.

HADITH

THE ARABIC language creates a balanced mind and enriches
human values.

'UMAR IBN AL-KHATTAB, *Editor*

AND THE king said to Hassan: We request you from your
kindness one of these jars of gold, for it will come in useful in
our work. And the boy Hassan replied and said: Take it. For I
am an Arab, and can an Arab refuse a request made by his guest?

FOLK TRADITION, *Campbell*

YOU ARE the finest breed who ever mounted a horse or a
camel,
And of the peoples of the world you are the ones the
palms of whose hands are always moist.

JARIR, *Editor*

HARITH BEN Keldah described the character of the Arabs before Khosraw Anúsharwán, in the following terms: 'Their minds are liberal, their hearts cheerful; their language is expressive, their tongues are eloquent, their pedigrees pure and genuine, their ancestors noble; the words flow from their mouths like arrows from the bow, but milder than the breezes of spring, and sweeter than honey; they feed the hungry in the time of need; they fight the strong in war; they do not permit that their high feelings should be hurt, that their neighbor should be injured, that their wives or daughters should be profaned, or, that the noble should be humbled.'

FOLK TRADITION, *Sprenger*

WE ARE beduin. We like people, or we don't like them.

SALIH AL-'ADAWI, *Stark*

THE ARABS have bravery, hospitable reception, fidelity, gallantry, generosity, responsibility to obligation, oratory, and a gift for explanation.

AL-TAWHIDI, *Damis*

[THE SETTLED ARABS SAY:] THE NOMADS ARE FULL OF WILY EVASIONS.

FOLK TRADITION, *Doughty*

ARABS ARE, withal, the quickest of peoples to follow the call to truth and righteousness. For their natures are relatively simple and free from the distorting effects of bad habits and evil ways; their only grave moral defect is their roughness, which indicating as it does a primitive and uncorrupted nature, can be rectified ... Arabs are, of all peoples, the least fit for exercising political domination. This is because they are more nomadic than other peoples, moving more freely in the deserts and, because of their simple and rough ways, standing in less need of cereals and other agricultural products. This makes them less dependent on others and therefore less ready to submit to authority.

IBN KHALDUN, *Issawi*

THE ARABS did not have a proper condition to follow as a pattern nor a Book to guide them. They are people of a poor land, deserted from mankind; everyone among them, in his loneliness, has need of his thought, his contemplation, and his mind. They knew that their livelihood came from the plants of the earth, so they marked each of them and attributed to each its type, and they knew the benefit that was in the fresh plant and the dry plant, and their growth cycles, and which were suitable for sheep and camels. Then they contemplated time and its succession and rendered it as spring, summer, mid-summer and winter. They knew that their drink was from the heavens, so they invented for them the constellations. And they were aware of the changing of time, so they made for it divisions of the year. They needed to spread out on the earth, so they made of the heavenly stars guides for the sections of the earth and its regions, and followed the land by means of them. And they made among themselves something which would prevent them from doing evil and which would make them desirous of the beautiful, by which they would avoid baseness and which would spur them on to excellent qualities, even to the extent that a member of their nation, though he be in any remote spot of the earth, describes these excellent qualities, not omitting a thing from his description, and he is immoderate in the censure of evil acts and condemns them at length. They do not discourse except in discussion which encourages good deeds, the preservation of the neighbor, the giving away of goods, and the setting up of commendable acts. Everyone of them achieves that by his mind and deduces it by his native intelligence and his thought, without learning or becoming well-mannered; instead, his natural disposition is well-bred and his mind is perceptive. This is why I said they are the most intelligent nation, because of the soundness of natural endowment, correctness of thought, and acuteness of understanding.

AL-TAWHIDI, *Damis*

GHAILÁN SON of Kharasha said to Ahnaf, 'What will preserve the Arabs from decline?' He replied, 'All will go well if they keep their swords on their shoulders and their turbans on their heads and ride on horseback and do not fall a prey to the fools' sense of honour.' 'And what is the fools' sense of honour?' 'That they regard forgiving one another as a wrong.'

AL-JAHIZ, *Nicholson*

HAPPINESS AND CONTENTMENT, GRIEF AND SORROW

RICHES ARE not from abundance of worldly goods, but from a contented mind.

HADITH

> FULL IS my sorrow now that you are dead,
> And I have thrown the dust upon your head.
> In other days I preached unendingly,
> But now, my little boy, you preach to me.

ABU AL-'ATAHIYA, *Baerlein*

THE ATTRIBUTE of patience is only surpassed by the zenithal station of contentment. The attribute of contentment encapsulates the essence of all love.

ABU AL-WAHID IBN ZAYD, *Editor*

O R RATHER my grief is like that of the she-dove, when she perceives the star of the waste, having dwelt in Yemen till some divine doom brought her to an arid land that had neither dew nor showers; and when she looks at Canopus, it reminds her of companions she had known in the land of Yemen, none of whom had ever dealt unkindly with her; and feeling her throat oppressed with regrets she begins to cry and grieve, alleviating by the emission of these sounds the grief which she feels for the dead; thinking that there is no escape from the confinement of the cage, she wishes that God would change her into a mewing day-cat, or moaning night-wolf; that she might escape by such deliverance from some of her troubles.

AL-MA'ARRI, *Margoliouth*

CAUSE ME not to covet what I cannot attain. How many who have coveted have failed to gain their wishes!

ARABIAN NIGHTS, *Lane*

HAPPINESS IS achieved if a man should have a dutiful and noble son, eat wholesome food, be married to a compatible woman, and be served by one who is fit to serve him.

FOLK TRADITION, *Editor*

LEAVE ME alone, O Umaimah – alone with my sleepless pain –
  alone with the livelong night and the wearily lingering stars;
It draws on its length of gloom; methinks it will never end,
  nor ever the Star-herd lead his flock to their folds of rest; –
Alone with a breast whose griefs, that roamed far afield by day,
  the darkness has brought all home: in legions they throng around.

AL-NABIGHAH, *Lyall*

LOVE

AND AMONG His Signs
Is this, that He created
For you mates from among
Yourselves, that ye may
Dwell in tranquillity with them,
And He has put love
And mercy between your (hearts):
Verily in that are Signs
For those who reflect.

QUR'AN 30: 21

HOW GLOWS mine heart for him whose heart to me is cold,
Who liketh ill my case and me in fault doth hold!
Why should I hide a love that hath worn thin my frame?

AL-MUTANABBI, Nicholson

VERILY I wonder – but how full is love of wonders:
  accompanied by anxieties and ardour and passion!

ARABIAN NIGHTS, Lane

YOU HAVE burdened the heart with what the body
     endureth not.
For the heart doth endure that which the body cannot.

AL-HALLAJ, *Editor*

BLAME ME no more, O comrades! but to-day
Quietly with me beside the howdahs stay.
Blame not my love for Zaynab, for to her
And hers my heart is pledged a prisoner.
Ah, can I ever think of how we met . . .
My song of other women was but jest:
She reigns alone, eclipsing all the rest.
Hers is my love sincere, 'tis she the flame
Of passion kindles – so, a truce to blame!

'UMAR IBN ABI RABI'A, *Nicholson*

TELL ME, for Love's sake, what is that flame which burns in my
     heart and devours my strength and dissolves my will?

KAHLIL GIBRAN, *Ferris*

HOW CAN a pain in the chest be softened?
The darts of death are closer than your hands.
Too much loss; too much want; absence. I tremble,
You can't come to me, I can't come to you.
Our love is a small bird tied by a child,
The bird sips the lake of death and the boy
Goes on with his game. He doesn't have the sense
To feel the bird's pain: and the wings can't fly.
I know a thousand roads, a thousand places,
But without a heart there is nowhere to go.

MAJNUN LAYLA, *al-Udhari and Wightman*

I HAVE lost my existence among mankind since your
    absence; for my heart loveth none but you.
Take my body, then, in mercy, to the place where you are
    laid; and there bury me by your side:
And if, at my grave, you utter my name, the moaning of
    my bones shall answer to your call.

ARABIAN NIGHTS, *Lane*

I LOVE her and she loves me,
And my he-camel loves her she-camel.

AL-MUNAKHKHAL AL-YASHKURI, *Editor*

OUR SIGNAL in love is the glance of our eyes; and every
   intelligent person understandeth the sign.
Our eyebrows carry on an intercourse between us: we
   are silent; but love speaketh.

ARABIAN NIGHTS, *Lane*

HOW MANY a man has been slain as I am slain, a martyr to
   white necks and rosy cheeks
And the eyes of wild cows – yet not like such eyes as have
   slaughtered this enslaved and wasted lover.
Blessings be upon the zephyr; O days when I trailed my
   skirts in Dár Athla, return!

AL-MUTANABBI, *Arberry*

LET HEART in fancy's realm roam as it will,
  The one whom first it loved it loveth still.
Though earth's fair habitations cast their spell,
  Man pineth still for where he first did dwell.

ABU TAMMAM, *Editor*

THE STRANGULATION of death is short, and ceaseth; but the
  disjunction of the beloved ever tortureth the heart.

ARABIAN NIGHTS, *Lane*

MAN, HAVE done! forget her, – one too far to comfort thee!
  Who would his love garner first let him sunder it.
Shed the love that fails thee. Strong be thou, and break
  with her.
Keep thy gifts for friendship, freed from thy wilderment.

LABID, *Blunt*

DEAR LOVE
'tis less than I have vowed
but let me gather in
and bring
all love
from earth and sea and sky;

then
let us to its equalling
that love,
when death has ravished us,
encase our shroud.

IBN AL-AHNAF, *Pound*

SHE IS the sun: her place is in heaven: comfort then the
   heart with a becoming patience:
For thou art not able to ascend unto her; nor is she able
   to descend unto thee.

ARABIAN NIGHTS, *Lane*

YES, BY Allah! I love the magic of your eyes, and yet I
   dread the weapons by which so many lovers fell.

BASHSHAR, *Bakalla*

UNSUMMONED IN the twilight they passed by,
So close to me they set my heart afire.

Why wonder that they stir up my desire?
Water but glimpsed makes thirsty men more dry.

AL-RADI BI-LLAH YAZID, *Morland*

TO LOVE is to kiss, to touch hand or arm
Or to send letters whose spells are stronger than
    witchcraft.

AL-WASHSA, *Hamori*

TRULY AT first sight I loved her, I who had slain her kin,
    ay, by the life of thy father, not in inconstancy.
Love, thou hast taken possession. Deem it not otherwise.
    Thou in my heart art the first one, first in nobility.

'ANTARAH, *Blunt*

THE HEART is contracted; and solicitude, extended; and
  the eye, sleepless; and the body, wearied;
And patience, cut short; and disjunction, continued; and
  reason, deranged; and the heart, snatched away.

ARABIAN NIGHTS, *Lane*

FOR THE ear is sometimes enamoured sooner than the
  eye.

BASHSHAR, *Bakalla*

DO NOT thou misprize me, thou Nowára. One am I
  binder of all love-knots, ay, and love's sunderer;
One who when love fails him, wails not long but flies from
    it;
  one whom one alone holds, hard death the hinderer.
What dost thou of mirth know, glorious nights, ah, how
    many –
  cold nor heat might mar them – spent in good
  company?

LABID, *Blunt*

O MY night, you grow ever more hateful, because of the
   love I bear towards a maiden with whom I have
   become enamoured.
A sparkling-eyed maiden is she; if she glances towards
   you, she makes you drunk by those two eyes.
The pattern of her discourse seems like meadow plots
   garbed in flowers, and as though beneath her tongue
   Harut sat breathing spells therein.
You might well imagine the body on which she gathers
   her garments to be all gold and scent.
It is as though she were the very coolness of drink itself –
   drink pure and suited to your breaking fast.
Be she a maiden of the jinn, a human girl, or somewhat
   between, she is a most splendid thing.
It is enough to say that I never heard tell of any
   complaint about the one I love,
Save the cry of one who would visit her: She has
   scattered sorrows all around for me,
Victim of passion for a ten-days space, and of very death
   for ten.

BASHSHAR, *Bakalla*

ENDLESSLY I search the skies
To find a star lit by your eyes;

I ask each traveller what land
Breathes fragrantly of you. I stand

Lonely, the wind upon my face
To tell what news there is, what trace ...

But when a song recalls your name
I walk the roads, endless and same,

Seeking a face that bears the sign
Of having seen you, one like mine.

ABU BAKR AL-TURTUSI, *Morland*

SHALL I ever meet Buthaina alone again,
Each of us full of love as a cloud of rain?
Fast in her net was I when a lad, and till
This day my love is growing and waxing still.

JAMIL, *Nicholson*

BY HIM who brings weeping and laughter who deals Death
and Life as He wills –
she left me to envy the wild deer that graze twain and
twain without fear!
Oh, love of her, heighten my heart's pain, and strengthen
the pang every night;
oh, comfort that days bring, forgetting – the last of all
days be thy tryst!
I marveled how swiftly the time sped between us, the
moment we met;
but when that brief moment was ended how wearily
dragged he his feet!

ABU SAKHR, *Lyall*

BEAUTY

HER CHEEKS make havoc with the lover's mind;
So many beauties are therein combined.
Hue of red roses tinting whitest skin:
Like tint of wine with water poured therein.
Or thin white robe beneath a red robe thin.

ABU FIRAS AL-HAMADHANI, *Margoliouth*

EVERY ROSE has its thorns.

FOLK TRADITION, *Editor*

HER GLANCE, like a gazelle's,
her throat, that of a white deer,
lips red as wine,
teeth white as sea foam.

Tipsiness made her languid.
The gold-embroidered figures
of her wrap swirled round her,
brilliant stars around the moon.

During the night love's hands
wrapped us in a garment of embraces
ripped open
by the hands of dawn.

IBN KHAFAJAH, *Franzen*

ALL BEAUTY is loved by the one who is able to perceive beauty, for the perception of beauty is a delight in itself, which is loved for its own sake, not for anything else ... It cannot be denied that where Beauty is perceived it is natural to love it and if it is certain that God is Beauty, He must be loved by that one to whom His Beauty and His Majesty are revealed. In God and in Him alone are all these causes of love combined and all things lovable found in their highest perfection. For it is to Him that man owes his very existence and the qualities by which he may attain to his perfection. He is the only real Benefactor and the Ultimate Cause of all benefits. If, where beauty is found, it is natural to love it, and if beauty consists in perfection, then it follows that the All-Beautiful, Who is Absolute Perfection, must be loved by those to whom His nature and attributes are revealed.

AL-GHAZZALI, *Smith*

BY HER plaits I wooed her, drew her face near to me,
　　won to her waist how frail-lined, hers of the ancle-rings.
Fair-faced she – no redness – noble of countenance,
　　smooth as of glass her bosom, bare with its necklaces.
Thus are pearls yet virgin, seen through the dark water,
　　clear in the sea-depths gleaming, pure, inaccessible.
Coyly she withdraws her, shows us a cheek, a lip,
　　she a gazelle of Wújra, – yearling the fawn with her.
Roe-like her throat slender, white as an áriel's,
　　sleek to thy lips up-lifted, – pearls are its ornament.
On her shoulders fallen thick lie the locks of her,
　　dark as the dark date-clusters hung from the palm-
　　branches.

IMRU' AL-QAYS, *Blunt*

'TWAS THEN her beauties first enslaved my heart –
Those glittering pearls and ruby lips, whose kiss
Was sweeter far than honey to the taste.
As when the merchant opes a precious box
Of perfume, such an odor from her breath
Comes toward me, harbinger of her approach;
Or like an untouched meadow, where the rain
Hath fallen freshly on the fragrant herbs
That carpet all its pure untrodden soil:
A meadow where the fragrant rain-drops fall
Like coins of silver in the quiet pools,
And irrigate it with perpetual streams;
A meadow where the sportive insects hum,
Like listless topers singing o'er their cups,
And ply their forelegs, like a man who tries
With maimèd hand to use the flint and steel.

'ANTARAH, *Palmer*

EVERY SLENDER-BELLIED maiden tenderer than wine, with
　a heart harder than granite,
Having tresses as though ambergris-drenched, mingled
　　with rose-water and aloes-wood,
Pitch-black as the raven, tangled and exceeding dark,
　　thick and naturally curly,
The wind is charged with musk from her plaits, and she
　　smiling to reveal white teeth, cool as hail-stones –
She has linked between Ahmad's body and sickness,
　　between his eyelids and sleeplessness.

AL-MUTANABBI, Arberry

IN BLACKNESS there is some virtue, if you observe its beauty
well, thy eyes do not regard the white or red. Were it not for
the black of the mole on a fair cheek, how would lovers feel
the value of its brilliancy. Were not musk black, it would not be
precious. Were it not for the black of night, the dawn would not
rise. Were it not for the black of the eye, where would be its
beauty? and thus it is, that the black ambergris has the purest
fragrance.

THE ROMANCE OF ANTAR, Hamilton

SHAME HITHERTO was wont my tears to stay,
But now by shame they will no more be stayed,
So that each bone seems through its skin to sob,
And every vein to swell the sad cascade.
Her beauty could dismay the young gazelle:
No wonder stricken me it hath dismayed.
She uncovered: pallor veiled her at farewell:
No veil 'twas, yet her cheeks it cast in shade;
So seemed they, while tears trickled over them,
Gold with a double row of pearls inlaid.
She loosed three sable tresses of her hair,
And thus of night four nights at once she made;
But when she lifted to the moon in heaven
Her face, two moons together I surveyed.

AL-MUTANABBI, *Nicholson*

FAMILY AND COMMUNITY LIFE

THY LORD hath decreed
That ye worship none but Him,
And that ye be kind
To parents. Whether one
Or both of them attain
Old age in thy life,
Say not to them a word
Of contempt, nor repel them
But address them,
In terms of honour.

And, out of kindness,
Lower to them the wing
Of humility, and say:
'My Lord! bestow on them
Thy Mercy even as they
Cherished me in childhood.'

QUR'AN 17: 23–24

A MAN is bound to do good to his parents, although they may have injured him.

HADITH

ALL GOD'S creatures are His family; and he is the most beloved of God who does most good to His creatures.

HADITH

HEAVEN LIETH at the feet of mothers.

HADITH

THE BEST way to behave towards one's friends is to care for them when they are in need or in poverty, to console them as much as possible without their having to ask for help, and to enquire after their relatives or dependents in the event of their death. For if a man is known for such behaviour everyone will seek his friendship and his friends will increase in number.

AL-FARABI, Editor

A MAN is a mirror in which his brother's likeness is seen.

FOLK TRADITION, Wortabet

Family and Community Life ↦ 147

KHALID IBN Safwan was asked 'Which of your friends do you prefer to others?' He said: 'He who fulfils the need of friendship, forgives my mistakes, and accepts my shortcomings.' Remember that amity, the spirit of brotherhood, and visiting one another are the basis of harmony and unity. Harmony and unity are the basis of strength, strength the basis of righteousness, and righteousness is an impregnable castle and a sound foundation, by which protection is provided against all harm, and through which wishes are fulfilled and goals are achieved.

FOLK TRADITION, *Editor*

IT IS related that Almighty God spoke to Moses using three thousand and five hundred words. The last words that God spoke were in answer to Moses's request: 'O God, direct me!', and God replied: 'We enjoin you to show kindness to your mother'. And God repeated these words seven times over, then added 'If your mother is well pleased with you, I shall be well pleased with you also; but if she is displeased with you, then I shall also be displeased with you.'

FOLK TRADITION, *Editor*

THE RIGHT attitude towards your fellow-man is that you should not lay burdens upon them according to your own desire, but rather burden yourself according to their desires.

AL-GHAZZALI, Smith

THE APPROVAL of God is dependent upon obtaining the approval of one's parents.

FOLK TRADITION, Editor

HE WHO resembles his father, wrongs not.

FOLK TRADITION, Steingass

IN HOUSE-HUNTING, search for the neighbour first.

FOLK TRADITION, Editor

HE WHO admonishes his brother in private gives advice and brings joy to his brother's heart, but he who admonishes his brother in public only exposes him and causes him much harm.

FOLK TRADITION, Editor

THE MAN of sense believes in fate and destiny, but not to the exclusion of prudence and foresight in human affairs: he unites his exertions for his own advantage, with his endeavours to promote that of others, and never seeks to benefit himself at the expense of his neighbour.

KALILA AND DIMNA, *Knatchbull*

GIVE HELP in whichever country you are and do not say 'I am a stranger'.

'UBAID IBN AL-ABRAS, *Editor*

I HAVE a country I'd never sell
Nor let anyone own. It has
Become the body of my soul.
If it was taken I would die.
People love the landscape of their youth.
When they think of home they recall
Their childhood and long to return.

IBN AL-RUMI, *al-Udhari and Wightman*

THE RULES governing all social relationships are: a smiling face, a joyous heart, refined character and polite manners.

FOLK TRADITION, *Editor*

A MAN was asked:
Who of your children is most beloved and receives most of your care?
He answered:
The one who is away, until he returns;
The one who is sick, until he recovers;
And the one who is young, until he grows.

FOLK TRADITION, *Editor*

THERE IS nothing better for a child than its mother's milk.

ARABIAN NIGHTS, *Lane*

FOR THERE may exist a brother of yours who is not born of your own mother.

FOLK TRADITION, *Editor*

I T IS related that 'Ali ibn Abi Taleb (may God bless his countenance!) said: 'Honour your kinsfolk, for they are the wings with which you soar; they help you to triumph, they elevate your station and champion you in times of difficulty. Honour the noble amongst them, visit the sick, make partners of them and bring relief to them when they are in distress.

FOLK TRADITION, Editor

THERE IS no peace for him who severs blood ties;
To sever family relationships breeds grief;
To desecrate what is holy eradicates all bounty;
To be undutiful towards one's parents results in misery,
    corrupts the community and diminishes our number.

AL-HARITH IBN KA'B, Editor

NAY, BUT our children in our midst, what else
    but our hearts are they, walking on the ground?
If but the breeze blow harsh on one of them,
    mine eye says 'no' to slumber, all night long!

HITTAN IBN AL-MU'ALLA OF TAYYI, Lyall

I T IS related that when the mother of al-Harith ibn al-Saouda' died she was a Christian, and that she had hidden this fact from everyone. Upon the news of her death many members of the household of the Prophet during the caliphate of 'Omar ibn al-Khattab assembled to attend the funeral. Al-Harith heard the womenfolk whispering among themselves, so he asked of them what the matter was. The women then told him that his mother had died a Christian, and that her necklace with a cross was still round her neck, but that she had kept her faith a secret. Whereupon al-Harith went to the people assembled outside his house for the funeral, and said to them: 'Please return to your homes; may God have mercy upon you, for my mother belongs to a people of another faith, and they are far more entitled than you or I to honour and bury her according to their own customs.'

AL-AGHANI, *Editor*

MEN AND WOMEN

O MANKIND! We created
You from a single (pair)
Of a male and a female,
And made you into
Nations and tribes, that
Ye may know each other
(Not that ye may despise
Each other).

QUR'AN 49: 13

WOMAN IS but man's full-sister.

HADITH

GOD ENJOINS you to treat women well, for they are your mothers,
daughters, and aunts.

HADITH

Know, o beloved, that man was not created in jest or at random, but marvelously made for some great end. Although he is not from everlasting, yet he lives for ever; and though his body is mean and earthly, yet his spirit is lofty and divine. When in the crucible of abstinence he is purged from carnal passions he attains to the highest, and in place of being a slave to lust and anger becomes endowed with angelic qualities. Attaining that state, he finds his heaven in the contemplation of Eternal Beauty, and no longer in fleshy delights. The Spiritual alchemy which operates this change in him, like that which transmutes base metals into gold, is not easily discovered.

AL-GHAZZALI, *Field*

THE DEFECTS of our social conditions disqualifies us from fully appreciating what great contributions women can make.

IBN RUSHD, *Editor*

GENTLENESS IS one of the noblest traits in a man's character.

FOLK TRADITION, *Wortabet*

THE BASE man, when he is hungry, begs, and when is fed,
    oppresses.

AL-HAMADHANI, *Prendergast*

AMONG THE obligations of the noble in character is to defend and
    honour women.

OUS IBN HARITHA, *Editor*

THE DEEDS of every man advise
What element within him lies:
The visual evidence is true –
Thou needst not seek another clue.

IBN HAZM, *Arberry*

A PIOUS man who had married an equally pious woman told
    her one day: 'I am an ill-tempered man.' She answered,
    'Worse than this would be the one who causes you to have
a bad temper!'

FOLK TRADITION, *Editor*

THE HEAD of the base man contains weakness, but does not contain understanding.

AL-HAMADHANI, *Prendergast*

VIRTUOUS WOMEN inspire righteous deeds.

FOLK TRADITION, *Editor*

HER SKIN is like silk, and her speech is soft, neither redundant nor deficient:
Her eyes, God said to them, Be – and they were, affecting men's hearts with the potency of wine.
May my love for her grow more warm each night, and cease not until the day of judgment!
The locks on her brow are dark as night, while her forehead shines like the gleam of morning.

ARABIAN NIGHTS, *Lane*

THE BEST of all men is the noble master; the protector of women; the bounteous and mild-tempered man; the experienced leader; the one who acts once he has made up his mind and gives generously if asked.

FOLK TRADITION, *Editor*

Men and Women ～ 157

BUT THE women those *howdahs* nestled,
More fair seemed they
Than statues, on marble chiselled,
Of Sukf, in the valley where Sájúm
Foams to the Persian bay.
Safely fended,
Softly tended,
With pearls and rubies and beads of gold
And gums of delicate odour in pyxes old,
Spicy musk and aloes and myrrh –
Sweet, oh, sweet is the breath of her
Who stole from thee, Sulaimà, my love away.

IMRU' AL-QAYS, *Nicholson*

THE INTELLIGENT man is quick to take a hint.

FOLK TRADITION, *Editor*

THE MOST virtuous of men is he whose humility is matched by his
sublime station, his detachment by the greatness of his
wealth, and his justice by his might and power.

FOLK TRADITION, *Editor*

THE BEST among you are those who are best to their womenfolk.

FOLK TRADITION, Sabbagh

AFAR FROM the voice of blame, her tent stands for all to see,
> when many a woman's tent is pitched in the place of scorn.

No gossip to bring him shame from her does her husband dread –
> when mention is made of women, pure and unstained is she.

The day done, at eve glad comes he home to his eyes' delight:
> he needs not to ask of her, 'Say, where didst thou pass the day?' –

And slender is she where meet, and full where it so beseems,
> and tall and straight, a fairy shape, if such on earth there be.

AL-SHANFARA, Lyall

AGE

T O EVERY young person who honoureth the old, on account of their age, may God appoint those who shall honour him in his years.

HADITH

HE DYES
his white hair black
in part,
believing some
will think him wise
and others
young.

IBN AL-RUMI, *Pound*

O, HOW strange are the deserted campsites and their long-gone inhabitants!
And how strangely time changes all!
The camel of youth walks slowly now; its once quick pace is gone; it is bored with travelling.

JARIR, *Jayussi*

THE ELDER is to the clan as the prophet to the nation.

FOLK TRADITION, *Levy*

O DEATH, nor violence nor flattery thou
Dost use; but when thou com'st, escape none may.
Methinks, thou art ready to surprise mine age,
As age surprised and made my youth his prey.
What ails me, World, that every place perforce
I lodge thee in, it galleth me to stay?
And O Time, how do I behold thee run
To spoil me? Thine own gift thou tak'st away!
O Time! inconstant, mutable art thou,
And o'er the realm of ruin is thy sway.

ABU AL-'ATAHIYA, *Nicholson*

IF A man be old and a fool, his folly is past all cure;
but a young man may yet grow wise and cast off his
foolishness.

ZUHAYR IBN ABI SULMA, *Lyall*

VANITY

H E WILL not enter hell, who hath faith equal to mustard seed in his heart; and he will not enter Paradise, who hath a single grain of pride, equal to a mustard seed in his heart.

HADITH

A LMIGHTY GOD offered the world so that you may seek eternal life ... The world is ephemeral but the life to come is eternal. Let not this ephemeral world fill you with vanity and distract you from that world which is eternal, prefer then that which is permanent to that which perishes. For the world does not last, and our end is to return to God ... Fear Almighty God ... be united and do not divide into factions 'And remember with gratitude God's favour unto you: for ye were enemies and He joined your hearts in love, so that by His Grace ye became brethren.'

'UTHMAN IBN AFFAN, *Editor*

NOT ALL thy hopes, O Man, canst thou attain
Some few are quickly won – the rest are vain,
   For favoring winds the venturing sailors pray;
Yet what they meet is calm or hurricane.

AL-MUTANABBI, *Beder*

THE ARROGANT man has no friends.

FOLK TRADITION, *Lunde and Wintle*

A NATURE is theirs – God gives the like to no other men –
   a wisdom that never sleeps, a bounty that never fails.
Their home is God's own land, His chosen of old; their
   faith is steadfast. Their hope is set on naught but the
   world to come.

AL-NABIGHAH, *Lyall*

HE WHO humbles himself before God is elevated by God above all
   men.

FOLK TRADITION, *Editor*

GENEROSITY, HOSPITALITY AND THE TREATMENT OF ONE'S GUEST

THOSE WHO spend (freely),
Whether in prosperity,
Or in adversity;
Who restrain anger,
And pardon (all) men; –
For God loves those
Who do good,

QUR'AN 3: 134

EVERY GOOD act is charity; and verily it is a good act to meet your brother with an open countenance, and to pour water from your own water-bag into his vessel.

HADITH

LET HIM who believes in God and the day of Judgement honour his guest.

HADITH

SO GENEROSITY is best
And noblest, when the thing possessed
Is rare, and he who makes the gift
Is famous for his stingy thrift.

IBN HAZM, *Arberry*

IT IS better to be a poor man than a miserly rich man.

AL-JAHIZ, *Editor*

GENEROSITY (MAY God establish the host of thy successes), adorns; but meanness (may fortune cast down the eye-lid of thy enviers), dishonours; the noble rewards, but the base disappoints; the princely entertains, but the niggard frights away; the liberal nourishes, but the churl pains; giving relieves, but deferring torments; blessing protects, and praise purifies; the honourable repays, for repudiation abases; the rejection of him who should be respected is error; a denial to the sons of hope is outrage; and none is miserly but the fool, and none is foolish but the miser; and none hoards but the wretched; for the pious clenches not his palms.

AL-HARIRI, *Chenery*

THE MISERLY man lives a life of poverty in this world, while in the next he will be judged as one of the rich.

'ALI IBN ABI TALEB, *Editor*

WHO GATHERS not friends by help, in many cases of need
  is torn by the blind beast's teeth, or trodden beneath
  its foot.
And he who his honor shields by the doing of a kindly
  deed
    grows richer; who shuts not the mouth of reviling, it
    lights on him.
And he who is lord of wealth and niggardly with his
  hoard,
    alone is he left by his kin; naught have they for him
    but blame.
Who keeps faith, no blame he earns, and that man whose
  heart is led
To goodness unmixed with guile gains freedom and peace
  of soul.

ZUHAYR IBN ABI SULMA, *Lyall*

DO NOT be ashamed to give little, for it is less than that, if you give nothing.

FOLK TRADITION, *Wortabet*

IF I be possessed of wealth and be not liberal, may my hand never be extended, nor my foot raised!
Shew me the avaricious who hath attained glory by his avarice, and the munificent who hath died through his munificence.

ARABIAN NIGHTS, *Lane*

GRACIOUSNESS IS the bounty of the gracious.

FOLK TRADITION, *Editor*

I WONDERED that one so noble as he should withhold;
Why should he withhold who, by giving, loses nothing?
The money-hoard is diminished by its gifts:
But the store of honour is not diminished.

IBN AL-RUMI, *Stark*

GIVE THE poor man who comes to thee a dole,
Scant though it be, nor frown away thy guest,
But raise for him a flame of ruddy crest
That frolics in the darkness like a foal!

AL-MA'ARRI, Nicholson

WE HASTED to open the door, and received him with
    welcome,
Saying to the servant, 'Hie! Hie! Bring whatever is ready!'
But the stranger said, 'By Him who brought me to your
    abode,
I will not taste of your hospitality, unless you pledge to me
That you will not permit me to be an incumbrance to
    you,
Nor impose on yourselves necessity of eating on my
    account.'

AL-HARIRI, Preston

OH GUEST, should you visit us, you would find us the guests and
    you the Master of the House.

FOLK TRADITION, Stark

HORSES, CAMELS AND THE DESERT

HE WHO treats his horse well, shall be well treated by God.

HADITH

GOD TOOK a handful of the south wind, and fashioned it into a
horse.

HADITH

A HORSE knows its rider best of all.

FOLK TRADITION, *Editor*

THE CARAVAN stopped for four days at a place called ath-
Thaniya outside Karak, where preparations were made for
entering the desert. Thence we journeyed to Ma'an, which
is the last town in Syria, and from Aqabat as-Sawan entered the
desert, of which the saying goes: 'He who enters it is lost, and he
who leaves it is born.'

IBN BATTUTA, *Gibb*

DURING A journey a man's character is weighed and revealed.

FOLK TRADITION, *Wortabet*

OR YOU might be upon a horse of A'waj lineage, one that will not readily stumble, with a body that might be made of gold, and hoofs of emerald, whose 'blaze' you would think a star of night, and his gallop the advance of a torrent. He does not compel his rider to say *háb* and *hab*, but dashes on with fiery energy. One that raises above him that reins him a neck tall as a palm-trunk, and rivals the north wind with his proud lineage; each time there comes in the way a wild herd or flock such a horse can set fetters on it. He is always fresh victual for his riders; he is bound to sustain them while in the desert. He is the enemy of the wild ass whom his morning visits frighten, as though he were a kite swooping from a high mountain, or glanced with the eyes of a hawk. He leaves the ostrich behind as though it were an orphan chick. He is too haughty to pick his way cautiously over the stones. The eyes of the enemy are intent upon his rider as upon a star in the heavens that shines to give them guidance. The points of the spears are not levelled at him; neither can he be reached save with the keenest gaze.

AL-MAʿARRI, *Margoliouth*

HONOUR LIVES in the manes of horses.

FOLK TRADITION, *Howarth and Shukrallah*

OF ALL the honoured places in the world
    There is none nobler than the saddle (of a horse)
And of all the boon companions in life
    There is none better than a book

ARABIC COUPLET, *Editor*

EVERY STEED is permitted one stumble.

FOLK TRADITION, *Sabbagh*

I SEVERED the cords thereof and away I wandered
On camel so fleet and strong she could ne'er be weary:
A stark beast – high she tosses her pair of riders –
Yet shrunken and worn with me on and off the saddle:
She stands as a castle built by a master-builder
Of Hájir with stones alike, each fitted squarely.
A wild-bull she . . .

LABID, *Nicholson*

Horses, Camels and the Desert ✤ 171

HOW MANY a noble steed like the glance in fast running
whom the imaginary phantom cannot surpass in nightly
travel,
whenever it travels at night, it is one of the bright stars,
and whenever it runs across the desert, is one of the
demons.
I do not know, when it is bound as I travel by night,
or when I ride it in the early morning of fighting,
whether it is a south wind being led to me from the side
or a north wind whose reins are in my left hand?

IBN KHAFAJAH, *al-Nowaihi*

CENTURIES AGO the Prophet Muhammad, while riding
through the desert, is said to have met a Bedouin leading
behind him a camel afflicted with a skin disease.
Distressed at the animal's suffering, he asked the Bedouin: 'What
are you doing to help the camel's condition?' 'Prophet of God, I
am praying to God to send a cure.' 'Pray on,' said the Prophet,
'but while you are about it, apply some of the black tar to the
camel's skin.'

FOLK TRADITION, *Editor*

GONE ARE they the lost camps, light flittings, long
sojournings
in Miná, in Gháula, Rijám left how desolate.
Lost are they. Rayyán lies lorn with its white torrent
beds,
scored in lines like writings left by the flood-water.
Tent-floors smooth, forsaken, bare of all that dwelt in
them,
years how long, the war-months, months too of peace-
pleasures.
Spots made sweet with Spring-rains, fresh-spilled from
the Zodiac,
showers from clouds down-shaken, wind-wracks and
thunder-clouds;
Clouds how wild of night-time, clouds of the dawn
darkening,
clouds of the red sunset, – all speak the name of her.

Here, in green thorn-thickets, does bring forth how
fearlessly;
here the ostrich-troops come, here too the antelopes.
Wild cows, with their wild calf-sucklings, standing over
them,
while their weanlings wander wide in the bare valleys.

Clean-swept lie their hearth-stones, white as a new
    manuscript
    writ with texts fresh-graven, penned by the cataracts,
Scored with lines and circles, limned with rings and
    blazonings,
    as one paints a maid's cheek point-lined in indigo.
All amazed I stood there. How should I make
    questionings?
    Dumb the rocks around me, silent the precipice,
Voices lost, where these dwelt who at dawn abandoning
    tent and thorn-bush fencing fled to the wilderness.

LABID, *Blunt*

AND OH, my love and yearning when at nightfall
    I saw her camels haste,
Until sharp peaks uptowered like serried swordblades
    And me Yamáma faced!
Such grief no mother-camel feels, bemoaning
    Her young one lost, nor she,
The grey-haired woman whose hard fate hath left her
    Of nine sons graves thrice three.

'AMR IBN KULTHUM, *Nicholson*

AND A mettlesome steed that never sped, but that the
   lightning trailed behind it from the striking of its hooves.
Dark of hue (it is), splitting the starless night with a
   blackness, between its eyes a blaze like the crescent
   moon.

'ANTARAH, *Arberry*

RODE I forth at day-dawn – birds in their nests asleep –
   stout on my steed, the sleek-coat, him the game-
   vanquisher.
Lo, he chargeth, turneth, – gone is he – all in one,
   like to a rock stream-trundled, hurled from its eminence.
Red-bay he, – his loin-cloth chafing the ribs of him
   Shifts as a rain-stream smoothing stones in a river-bed.
Hard is he, – he snorteth loud in the pride of him,
   fierce as a full pot boiling, bubbling beneath the lid.

IMRU' AL-QAYS, *Blunt*

SHOW PATIENCE and love towards your horse, for the horse is
   endowed with power and beauty.

FOLK TRADITION, *Editor*

TO BRING him there, he wants a stout she-camel which,
  though fatigued, loses not her wonted speed and pace;
One that largely bedews the bone behind her ear when
  she sweats, one that sets herself to cross a trackless
  unknown wilderness;
Scanning the high grounds with eyes keen as those of a
  solitary white oryx, when stony levels and sand-hills
  are kindled (by the sun);
Big in the neck, fleshy in the hock, surpassing in her
  make the other daughters of the sire;
Thick-necked, full-cheeked, robust, male-like, her flanks
  wide, her front (tall) as a milestone . . .
Onager-like is she; her side slabbed with firm flesh, her
  elbow-joint far removed from the ribs;
Her nose aquiline; in her generous ears are signs of
  breeding plain for the expert to see, and in her cheeks
  smoothness . . .
Though she be not trying, she races along on light slender
  feet that skim the ground as they fall,
With tawny hock-tendons – feet that leave the gravel
  scattered and are not shod so that they should be kept
  safe from the blackness of the heaped stones.

KA'B IBN ZUHAYR, *Nicholson*

THREE TYPES of service shame not a Bedouin: service rendered to
his home, his horse and his guest.

FOLK TRADITION, *Editor*

WHITE AS the morning-star
At sunrise, proud and cold,
His saddle gleaming gold,
He steps before me into battle ...
    Then how envious are
The Captains. One cries loud:
'Who has flung the Pleiades
For bridle on the dawn?
And with the half-moon for a saddle
Tames the lightning down?'

ABU SALT UMAYYA, *Morland*

OH, FOR the beauty of this dark bay horse.
Lightning cannot match it when running on its course.
By virtue of its speed, the sun cannot succeed
    to throw its shadow on solid ground.

FOLK TRADITION, *Anonymous*

AY, WELL is that custom known, a usage that time has
    proved when lances are laid in rest on withers of
    steeds arow –
Of steeds in the spear-play skilled, with lips for the fight
    drawn back, their bodies with wounds all scarred,
    some bleeding and some half-healed.
And down leap the riders where the battle is strait and
    stern, and spring in the face of Death like stallions
    amid the herd;
Between them they give and take deep draughts of the
    wine of doom as their hands ply the white swords, thin
    and keen in the smiting-edge.

AL-NABIGHAH, *Lyall*

THREE OF God's bounties are a virtuous wife, a thoroughbred
    horse and a sharp sword.

FOLK TRADITION, *Editor*

BECOMING A LEADER

RULERSHIP, AUTHORITY, STATECRAFT AND LEADERSHIP

IT IS He Who hath made
You (His) agents, inheritors
Of the earth: He hath raised
You in ranks, some above
Others: that He may try you
In the gifts He hath given you:
For thy Lord is quick
In punishment: yet He
Is indeed Oft-forgiving,
Most Merciful.

QUR'AN 6: 165

THE BEST of your rulers are those whom you love and who love you, who invoke God's blessings upon you and you invoke His blessings upon them. And the worst of your rulers are those whom you hate and who hate you, and whom you curse and who curse you.

HADITH

A KING is deceived in the expectations which he forms from the exercise of arbitrary power; for a mild and gentle government is alone consistent with the dictates of prudence and good sense.

KALILA AND DIMNA, *Knatchbull*

SHOW KINDNESS to your people and they will love you;
Be humble before them and they will elevate you;
Look on them with a friendly face and they will obey you;
Do not acquire any privileges which exclude them and
    they will make you their master;
Honour their young as you honour their elderly;
And their elderly will in turn honour you,
While their young will be nurtured to grow in your love;
Be generous with whatever you possess;
Protect your womenfolk;
Esteem your neighbour;
Support him who seeks your assistance;
Be bountiful to your guest;
And be quick to answer the one who cries for help.

IBN AL-ISBA 'AL-ADWANI, *Editor*

A GOAT was standing on a roof and abusing a wolf who was standing down below. The wolf replied, 'It is not thou who art abusing me, but it is the place whereon thou standest.'

FOLK TRADITION, *Budge*

Y OUR POSITION [as secretary] with regard to rulers is that (you are) the ears through which they hear, the eyes through which they see, the tongues through which they speak, and the hands through which they touch ... If any one of you be appointed to an office, or if some matter that concerns God's children be turned over to one of you, he should think of God and choose obedience to Him. He should be kind to the weak and fair to those who have been wronged. All creatures are God's creatures. He loves most those who are kindest to His children.

'ABD AL-HAMID AL-KHATIB, *Rosenthal*

THE WORST of rulers is he who inspires fear in the heart of the innocent.

FOLK TRADITION, *Editor*

THREE THINGS sustain dominion: compassion, justice and generosity.

FOLK TRADITION, Editor

EVEN IF a ruler is just, half of the inhabitants of his domain will always remain enemies to his reign.

FOLK TRADITION, Editor

HE WHO leads people and manages their affairs is in need of a wide chest and he must gird himself with patience and bear up with the want of culture of the common people; he must make the ignorant understand and satisfy the man against whom the decision has gone and who has been denied his request by pointing out whence he has been denied it; for since people are not universally satisfied, even if all the causes of satisfaction have been put together for their benefit, much less will they be satisfied if some have been withheld from them. And they do not accept obvious excuses, even less dubious ones. And your brother is he who tells you the truth and is grieved for you, not he who follows you in your passion and afterwards disappears from you without bringing you near.

IBN QUTAYBA, Horovitz

A KING said to his son, 'The pleasure of forgiving is followed by praiseworthy consequences, while the satisfaction derived from one's thirst for revenge is followed by regret and the pain of censure.'

FOLK TRADITION, *Editor*

> THUS THE tribes were trysted; nor failed we the provident
>   to name one, a wise man, fair-tongued, as judge for
>   them,
> One who the spoil portioned, gave to each his just
>   measure,
>   spake to all unfearing, gave or refused to give,
> A just judge, a tribe-sheykh, wise, fair-worded, bountiful,
>   sweet of face to all men, feared by the warriors.

LABID, *Blunt*

HE WHO does not possess a thing cannot give it.

FOLK TRADITION, *Editor*

FEAR GOD in regard to the lowest class in society, who are helpless, poor and miserable. You are responsible to God, for He entrusted them to you. The distant should receive as much as those who are near. Give each his due, and if you think this is beneath your dignity, do not make excuses. You will not be forgiven if you ignore minor matters to concentrate on those which seem important. Look into the affairs of those who are so weak that they cannot reach you. Appoint God-fearing and humble persons to bring their affairs before you. Give attention to the helpless orphans and the young who would never beg. The burden of responsibility on a viceroy is indeed a heavy one.

'ALI IBN ABI TALEB, *Waddy*

A BEDOUIN was asked, 'How has that man become the lord of his people?' He answered, 'Through noble ancestry and on account of his sagacity.'

FOLK TRADITION, *Editor*

YOUR NEED for a leader who acts is greater than your need for a leader who chats.

'UTHMAN IBN AFFAN, *Editor*

Rulership, Authority, Statecraft and Leadership ☙ 185

As for the requirements of good rule, they are that the ruler defend his subjects and be generous towards them. Defence is indeed the *raison d'être* of rulership, while generosity is one aspect of the ruler's gentleness towards his subjects and one means by which he can increase their welfare; it is also one of the chief ways of gaining their affection.

IBN KHALDUN, *Issawi*

Let him who appoints himself to lead others as teacher and *Imam* begin by teaching his own self, and let him correct his own conduct before he starts correcting others with his tongue.

'ALI IBN ABI TALEB, *Editor*

The most miserable of rulers is he who brings misery to his own people.

'UMAR IBN AL-KHATTAB, *Editor*

Howsoever you are, so shall you be ruled.

FOLK TRADITION, *Editor*

K NOW, THEN, that the use of the ruler to his subjects lies not in his person, his fine figure or features, his wide knowledge, his excellent penmanship or the sharpness of his intellect, but solely in his *relationship to them*. For kingship and rule are relative terms, implying a certain relation between two objects: the ruler being the possessor of his subjects and the manager of their affairs. The ruler is, then, he who has subjects and the subjects are those who have a ruler, the ruler's relationship to his subjects being one of possession.

IBN KHALDUN, *Issawi*

BE NOT so lenient as to be squeezed dry, nor so rigid as to be broken.

FOLK TRADITION, *Editor*

T HE VOICE of wisdom, said he [the king] to himself, has pronounced four things to be disgraceful to kings; anger . . . avarice . . . falsehood . . . and obscene conversation.

KALILA AND DIMNA, *Knatchbull*

THE TRIBES of the desert are kept off from each other by the authority of their chiefs and elders, whom they respect greatly. For the defence of their encampments against a foreign enemy, each tribe has a troop of warriors and knights famous for their prowess; but they would not make a firm resistance and defence unless they were united by kinship and a feeling of solidarity (*'asabíya*). That is what renders them so strong and formidable. *Esprit de corps* and devotion to one's kin is of supreme importance. The affection which God has put in the hearts of His servants towards those of their own flesh and blood is inherent in human nature: it leads them to help and succour one another and inspires their foes with terror.

IBN KHALDUN, *Nicholson*

BEWARE OF the company of Kings, for he who befriends them loses his wealth to them, while he who fosters enmity towards them loses his head.

ABU AL-'ALI AL-SAGHA'I, *Editor*

A S THE doctor treats any sick member only in accordance with its relation to the whole body and the members adjacent to it and connected with it, since he treats it with a cure by which he affords it health whereby the whole body benefits, and the members adjacent to it and connected with it benefit, so the ruler of the city must necessarily rule the affair of each part of the city, small, like one man, or great, like a household, and treat it and afford it good in relation to the whole city and each of the other parts of the city, by seeking to do what affords that part a good which does not harm the whole city nor any of its parts, but a good from which the city as a whole benefits, and each of its parts according to its degree of usefulness to the city. And just as when the doctor does not observe this, aims at providing health to a particular member and treats it without regard to the condition of the other members near it, or treats it with what is bad for all the other members, and affords it health but thereby does something which does not benefit the body as a whole nor the members adjacent to it and connected with it, that member is impaired, as well as the connected members, and the evil permeates the other members, till the whole body is corrupted, so the city also.

AL-FARABI, *Dunlop*

HE WHO rules justly feels secure and sleeps peacefully.

FOLK TRADITION, *Editor*

NOW THE excellence of rulership arises out of gentleness. For if the king is harsh, prone to inflict heavy punishments, always searching for the defects of his subjects and enumerating their misdeeds, they will be seized by terror and humiliation and will seek to protect themselves from him by lying, trickery and deceit until these qualities become ingrained in them and ruin their character. They may desert him in wartime, thus imperilling the country or else may conspire to kill him, ruining the state and its defences. And if such a condition should persist, their solidarity will be weakened and with it the very basis of protection of the state.

IBN KHALDUN, *Issawi*

COURAGE AND CHIVALRY

WHEN GOES forth the host to war, above them in circles
  wheel
    battalions of eagles, pointing the path to battalions more;
Their friendship is old and tried, fast comrades, in foray
  bred
    to look unafraid on blood, as hounds to the chase well
    trained.
Behold them, how they sit there, behind where their
  armies meet,
    watching with eyes askance, like elders in gray furs
    wrapt,
Intent; for they know full well that those whom they
  follow, when
    the clash of the hosts shall come, will bear off the
    victory . . .
Their sandals are soft and fine, and girded with chastity,
    they welcome with garlands sweet the dawn of the
    Feast of Palms.
There greets them when they come home full many a
  handmaid fine,
    and ready, on trestles, hang the mantles of scarlet silk.

Yea, softly they wrap their limbs, well-knowing of wealth
  and ease,
    in rich raiment, white-sleeved, green at the shoulder –
    in royal guise.

AL-NABIGHAH, *Lyall*

AS THE warm sun was he in wintry weather,
'Neath the Dog-star shade and coolness together;
Spare of flank, yet this in him showed not meanness;
Open-hearted, full of boldness and keenness;
Firm of purpose, cavalier unaffrighted –
Courage rode with him and with him alighted;
In his bounty a bursting cloud of rain-water;
Lion grim when he leaped to the slaughter.

TA'ABBATA SHARRA, *Nicholson*

SO COWARDS, rarely brave in war,
Are more applauded when they are
Than heroes, who sustain all day
The heat and fury of the fray.

IBN HAZM, *Arberry*

I HAVE abused fortune, but how can she humiliate such as me! I too that have a spirit would cut down mountains. I am the warrior of whom it is said, he tended the he and she camels of his tribe. When I assaulted Kendeh and Tey, their hands brandishing the long spears, with armies, that when I thought of them I imagined the whole earth filled with men; and as their hardy steeds trampled our lands, whilst you might see them talking and exulting, 'twas then their steeds fled away horrified at me, and the redoubled thrusts that gored them as they sought the fight. The noble hero feels no fatigue; him no challenger need call to the combat. It was the slave alone that drove back the horsemen whilst the flame of battle was blazing, – then speeded away their troops in terror of my arm, – light they fled, burthened though they had been. Crushing were the stamps and tramplings on their necks, and the horse shoes dashed and pounded their skulls. How many warriors were laid low by my sword, whilst they tore, in very rage, their hands with their teeth. I rescued the maidens and virgins, and not one did I leave but bereft of sense. Mine is a spirit for every enterprise, high is my fame, exalted is my glory.

THE ROMANCE OF ANTAR, *Hamilton*

WISE COUNSEL should be your first choice, the second should be
  bravery.

FOLK TRADITION, *Sabbagh*

LEARN, MÁLIK'S daughter, how
I rush into the fray,
And how I draw back only
At sharing of the prey.

I never quit the saddle,
My strong steed nimbly bounds;
Warrior after warrior
Have covered him with wounds.

Full-armed against me stood
One feared of fighting men:
He fled not oversoon
Nor let himself be ta'en.

'ANTARAH, *Bakalla*

IF WAR thou hast wrought and brought on me,
No laggard I with arms outworn.
Whate'er betide, I make to flow
The baneful cups of death at morn.

When spear-heads clash, my wounded man
Is forced to drag the spear he stained.
Never I reck, if war must be,
What Destiny hath preordained.

Donning war's harness, I will strive
To fend from me the shame that sears.
Already I thrill and my lust is roused
For the shock of the horsemen against the spears!

MURRA OF SHAIBAN, *Nicholson*

I FEAR that I might die in bed, and hope for a death under the
points of full spears.

FOLK TRADITION, *Bakalla*

THESE ARE some of the signs of the ones who follow the path of *Futuwah* [Sufi chivalry]:

Distribute freely from your property and help others from the rank that has been bestowed upon you. Do not expect appreciation or praise; give when you are asked to show your wealth and your position; serve your guests with your own hands, and serve and give lovingly, not grudgingly. Feed your friends from your own food and show them respect; meet the needs of your brethren with your property and your very life; respond to others' faults with kindness; visit those who do not visit you; be humble and avoid arrogance; avoid self-love and do not think highly of your state. Do good consistently to your mother and father; visit your kin; do not see the faults of others, keep secret their wrongdoings, and advise them only when no one can hear; pray for the sinners and pardon their wrongdoings. Feel the evil and the terror of your ego, and the shame of going along with it. Show consideration to people and compassion, kindness, and good to the faithful and the Muslims. Pity the poor and be compassionate toward the rich; be modest before men of knowledge; discern the truth in what you hear and accept it. Save your tongue from lies and slander, save your ears from error, and save your eyes from looking at the unlawful. Be sincere and pure in your actions, be straight in your states. See what is good and beautiful in the Creation; escape from the evil and befriend the good. Turn away from the worldly and face Allah. Leave your wants; throw away the desire to be praised for your worldly achievement. Be honored by the company of the poor. Avoid respecting the rich for their riches; the real wealth is to be with one's Lord. Be thankful for what is given to you. Tell the truth without fearing anybody. Offer thanks for things in which you find joy, and be patient with the difficulties that you have to tolerate. Flee from the curse of disloyalty and keep others' secrets. When you are with company, sit at a place below that which is due to your rank. Give up your rights, while fully upholding the rights of others. Educate your ego. Abide by Allah's prohibitions when you are by yourself. Consult your friends in every matter. Trust in Allah when you are in need. Do not be ambitious. Show respect to the devout, show kindness to the sinful. Do not cause discomfort to anyone; let your outer self be the same as your inner self. Be friends with the friend of your friend and enemies with the enemy of your friend. No matter how far away your friend is, be with him.

MUHAMMAD IBN AL-HUSAYN AL-SULAMI, *al-Halveti*

HONOUR AND NOBILITY

BEHOLD, THY Lord said
To the angels: 'I am
About to create man
From clay:

'When I have fashioned him
(In due proportion) and breathed
Into him of My spirit,
Fall ye down in obeisance
Unto him.'

QUR'AN 38: 71–72

GOD HAS created man in his wisdom and mercy, has raised him to excellence and honour, and has put into his power the means of happiness in this world, and of avoiding punishment in the next.

KALILA AND DIMNA, *Knatchbull*

A SUMMER'S night I met my girl on the path
That leads straight to her dwelling and straight to my
    tent.

We were alone, we two, without watchers or informers,
Far from the tribe, far from jealous eyes and spying ears
    and harming tongues.

I laid my face on the ground, my brow a footstool for my
    girl.
She said: 'Open your heart with joy, we are without
    watchers;
Come press your lips to my veil.'

But my lips would not consent to it.
I felt that I had two honours to guard,
My girl's and mine.

And, as was my desire, we were all night together,
Near to each other, far from the tribe and spying eyes.

And it seemed that I was master
Of all the kingdoms of the world, and that the elements
Obeyed me as slaves.

IBN AL-FARID, *Mathers*

A MAN honours himself by not displaying all the knowledge he has
   acquired.

FOLK TRADITION, *Editor*

HONOUR LIES in the mind and in acquired worth, not in origins
   and noble birth.

FOLK TRADITION, *Levy*

IF THOU ask a favour, ask it of the generous, who hath
      known,
   unceasingly, riches and opulence;
For asking of the generous is productive of honour, and
      asking of the base is productive of disgrace.
When abasement is a thing not to be avoided, meet with
      it by asking of the great.
Thine honouring the great is no abasement of thyself: it
      is only abasement to honour the [unworthy].

ARABIAN NIGHTS, *Lane*

WHEN A man's honour is not defiled by baseness, then
every cloak he cloaks himself in is comely;
And if he has never constrained himself to endure
despite, then there is no way (for him) to (attain)
goodly praise.

AL-SAMAW'AL, Arberry

THE DEATH of a man is better than his living in the abode
of contempt between the slanderer and the envier.

ARABIAN NIGHTS, Lane

THAT HE who his own face befouleth none else shall
honour him.

ZUHAYR IBN ABI SULMA, Blunt

PLAINLY (SAY the Arabs) the men of former ages were of great
stature.

FOLK TRADITION, Doughty

ARISE, O my mother's sons, and breast with your steeds
    the night,
For truly the love I bear is kinder to some less kin.
'Tis all ready that ye want for going your ways aright:
The saddles on, girths tied fast, and moonlight to journey
    in.

And somewhere the noble find a refuge afar from scathe,
The outlaw a lonely spot where no fires of hatred burn;
Oh, never a prudent man, night-faring in hope or fear,
Hard pressed on the face of earth, but still he hath room
    to turn.

To me now, in your default, are comrades a wolf untired,
A sleek leopard, and a fell hyena with shaggy mane.
Yet I, when the foremost charge, am bravest of all the
    brave;
But if they with hands outstretched are seizing the booty
    won,
The slowest am I whenas most quick is the greedy knave.

AL-SHANFARA, *Nicholson*

PEACE AND WAR

BUT IF the enemy
Incline towards peace,
Do thou (also) incline
Towards peace, and trust
In God: for He is the One
That heareth and knoweth
(All things).

QUR'AN 8: 61

SHALL I not inform you of a better act than fasting, alms, and
prayers? Making peace between one another: enmity and
malice tear up heavenly rewards by the roots.

HADITH

AS TWO sticks often ignite a fire
War may start with words of ire.

FOLK TRADITION, *Editor*

THERE IS a poem popular amongst the people which they put into the mouth of Adam when he mourned, it runs:

'The country is altered, and all that is in it.

The whole earth has changed for the worse.

All that has life and colour is different; and the sea has lost its lovely appearance.

The inhabitants have turned the produce of the fields into poison and bitterness, and an enemy infests us.

The cursed has not overlooked man, as we perceive; for Cain has cruelly slain Hábíl, and that amiable countenance is withered.

My lot is to shed tears; for Hábíl rests in the grave.

I see a life before me full of sorrow, and all that I may meet in it will be gloomy.'

AL-MASUʻDI, *Sprenger*

TO OVERCOME the weak has all the shame of a defeat.

FOLK TRADITION, *Wortabet*

DESTRUCTION IS easier than construction, and division than composition.

AL-MASUʻDI, *Howarth and Shukrallah*

HOW EVIL a thing is war, that bows men to shameful rest!
War burns away in her blaze all glory and boasting of
   men:
Naught stands but the valiant heart to face pain – the
   hard-hoofed steed –
The ring-mail set close and firm, the nail-crowned helms
   and the spears;
And onset, again after rout, when men shrink from the
   serried array –
Then, then, fall away all the vile, the hirelings! and
   shame is strong!
War girds up her skirts before them, and evil unmixed is
   bare.
For their hearts were for maidens veiled, not for driving
   the gathered spoil:
Yea, evil the heirs we leave, sons of Yakshar and al-
   Laksh!

But let flee her fires who will, no flinching for me, son of
   Kais!
O children of Kais! stand firm before her! gain peace or
   give:
Who seeks flight before her fear, his Doom stands and
   bars the road.

Away! Death allows no quitting of place, and brands are
    bare!
What is life for us, when the uplands and valleys are ours
    no more?
Ah, where are the mighty now? the spears and generous
    hands?

SA'D IBN MALIK, *Lyall*

MAGNANIMITY TO captives, and mercy to the fallen, are a hymn of
praise to God for victory.

FOLK TRADITION, *Wortabet*

FALSEHOOD HATH so corrupted all the world
That wrangling sects each other's gospel chide;
But were not hate Man's natural element,
Churches and mosques had risen side by side.

AL-MA'ARRI, *Nicholson*

THE ETERNAL conflicts are: the conflicts between body and soul; faith and reason; male and female; master and servant; true principle and selfish desire; man and nature; and between you and me.

AMEEN RIHANI, Editor

VIOLENCE IS infamous: its result is ever uncertain, and no one can act justly when actuated by hatred.

THE ROMANCE OF ANTAR, Hamilton

AWARENESS OF SELF

THE MAN *par excellence* is he
Who is self-sufficient wherever he may be.

AL-TUGHRA'I, Editor

I HAVE heard many sermons and had many counsels, but I have heard no preacher so effective as my grey hairs, and no counselor so effectual as the voice of my own conscience.

FOLK TRADITION, Wortabet

I AM the fountain of wonders.
In trickery I am the possessor of high degrees.
In truth, I am the camel's hump.
In falsehood I am its withers.
Alexandria is my home, an aimless
Wanderer am I on God's earth.
In the monastery I am an abbot,
In the mosque, a monk.

AL-HAMADHANI, Prendergast

THE MOST profitable thing for a man is to know his own worth.

KALILA AND DIMNA, *Knatchbull*

BEWARE OF envy, for it shows itself in you, not in him whom you envy.

FOLK TRADITION, *Wortabet*

NOT IN my people have I found honour, but rather they in
   me; and my boast is in myself, not in my ancestors,
In whom indeed is the pride of every true Arab, and the
   refuge of the wrongdoer, and the succour of the
   outcast.
If I am conceited, it is the conceit of an amazing man who
   has never found any surpassing himself.
I am the twin of bounty, the master of rhyme, the bane of
   my enemies, the baffled rage of the envious;
I am amongst a people – may God save them in His
   mercy – a stranger, like Sálih amongst Thamúd.

AL-MUTANABBI, *Arberry*

TRUE HONOUR lies in sound reason and courteous manners and
not in one's family lineage.

'ALI IBN ABI TALEB, *Editor*

THESE ARE our works which we have left behind
They speak on our behalf when we have passed away.

FOLK TRADITION, *Editor*

ALL MEN know us of old in Maád, the tribesmen,
   when our tents we have built in the open pastures,
Feasters are we of men with the men that love us,
   slayers are we of men, the men that hate us;
Rightful lords of the plain, to forgive and welcome;
   where we will we have pitched. Who has dared gainsay
   us?

'AMR IBN KULTHUM, *Blunt*

FOR THE horsemen know me, and the night, and the desert,
and the sword and lance, and the paper and pen.

AL-MUTANABBI, *Arberry*

ADVICE AND COUNSEL

IN ADVISING his friends Abu Turab al-Nakhshabi asked them to
heed the following precepts:
Do not be unjust if you are unjustly treated
Do not be complacent if you are praised
Do not be disappointed if you are criticized
Do not be angry if you are questioned
Do not betray anyone if you are betrayed.

FOLK TRADITION, *Editor*

IT IS an old saying, that a king, who is intoxicated with power,
is in his conduct little better than a child, and can only be
weaned from the error into which he has fallen by the
admonition of wise counsellors, whose duty it is to give weight to
their exhortations by the firm and dignified language in which
they are delivered, and to repair the moral infirmities of the
sovereign, by inculcating a respect for the laws of equity and
justice; imitating in their conduct the practice of the physician,
whose business it is to preserve the body in its sound state, or in
case of disease to restore it to health by judicious treatment of
his patient.

KALILA AND DIMNA, *Knatchbull*

I F YOU ask a favour of a man of noble nature, allow him time to think, because he will think only of what good he can do. But if you ask it of a man of ignoble nature, then persuade him to act quickly so that he may not succumb to the dictates of his nature and deny you what you have asked.

FOLK TRADITION, Editor

T HE MAN of the world is not supposed to live entirely for himself; if he has learning, he is bound to instruct the ignorant; if he has wealth, it is his duty to assist the needy; and in his intercourse with mankind, taking compassion on the frailties of human nature, he must be kind and indulgent to the faults which he shares in common with others, and not imitate the conduct of the blind man, who blamed his friend for having the same imperfection.

KALILA AND DIMNA, Knatchbull

T HERE ARE three types of people in the world. The capable person is one who can make decisions and seek advice. The half-capable person is one who can reach decisions but neglects to seek advice. The incapable person is one who can neither make decisions nor seek advice.

FOLK TRADITION, Editor

TRUST NOT a person in whose heart thou hast made anger
to dwell; nor think his anger hath ceased.
Verily, the vipers, which are smooth to the touch, and
shew graceful motions, hide mortal poison.

ARABIAN NIGHTS, *Lane*

IF YOU should be on your guard with your enemy once, then
you should be on your guard with your friend a thousand
times; for a friend when he ceases to be a friend may know
best how to inflict harm upon you.

FOLK TRADITION, *Editor*

FLEE WITH thy life if thou fearest oppression, and leave the
house to tell its builder's fate.
Thou wilt find, for the land that thou quittest, another:
but no soul wilt thou find to replace thine own.

ARABIAN NIGHTS, *Lane*

EXHORTATION GIVEN before all men is a reproof.

FOLK TRADITION, *Levy*

Advice and Counsel ↬ 213

T HERE ARE seven men whose counsel a wise man never seeks: an ignorant man, an enemy, a jealous man, a hypocrite, a coward, a miserly man, and a capricious man, because

the ignorant man misleads you,

the enemy wishes you harm,

the jealous man desires your impoverishment,

the hypocrite seeks to please others,

the coward only knows how to escape,

the miser is only interested in accumulating wealth and has no other course to follow,

the capricious man is obsessed by his own whims and caprices and cannot be free of them.

FOLK TRADITION, *Editor*

THERE IS none in thy time whose friendship thou shouldst covet; nor any intimate who, when fortune is treacherous, will be faithful.

Live then apart, and rely upon no man: I have given thee, in these words, good advice, and sufficient.

ARABIAN NIGHTS, *Lane*

THE INTELLIGENT person is one who protects the interests of his brothers, not one who follows his brothers' desires.

'ABDA, SISTER OF ABU SULAYMAN AL-DARANI, *Cornell*

EVEN THE advice of age I spurned when it censured me. Yet age is far above suspicion in its counsel.

AL-BUSIRI, *Sperl and Shackle*

AVOID THE sea, for the one who ventures into it is lost while the one who comes out of it is newly born.

FOLK TRADITION, *Editor*

I HEARD three sayings more wonderful than any I have ever heard. The first is the saying of Hassán son of Abú Sinán – 'Nothing is easier than abstinence from things unlawful: if aught make thee doubt, leave it alone.' The second is the saying of Ibn Sírín – 'I have never envied any one any thing.' The third is the saying of Muwarrik al-'Ijlí – 'Forty years ago I asked of God a boon which He has not granted, and I have not despaired of obtaining it.' They said to Muwarrik, 'What is it?' He replied, 'Not to meddle with that which does not concern me.'

AL-JAHIZ, *Nicholson*

MAY GOD save you from suspicion,
Protect you against embarrassment,
Allow you to gain knowledge and pursue what is true.
May He instil in you circumspection,
Adorn your vision with justice,
Permit you to taste the sweetness which is in
    righteousness,
Fill your heart with the power of Truth,
Infuse your breast with the solace of certainty,
Banish from your self the degradation of despair.

FOLK TRADITION, *Editor*

ART AND LEARNING

LEARNING, KNOWLEDGE AND ITS VIRTUES

HE GRANTETH wisdom
To whom He pleaseth;
And he to whom wisdom
Is granted receiveth
Indeed a benefit overflowing.

QUR'AN 2: 269

WHOSO PURSUETH the road of knowledge, God will direct him to the road of Paradise; and verily the angels spread out their arms to welcome the searcher after wisdom, and all things in Heaven and Earth ask grace for him: for the pre-eminence of a learned man over a mere worshipper is as the full moon above the stars.

HADITH

IT IS the duty of every believer, man or woman, to seek knowledge.

HADITH

AN HOUR'S contemplation is better than a year's [prayerful] adoration.

HADITH

ACQUIRE KNOWLEDGE. It enableth its possessor to distinguish right from wrong; it lighteth the way to Heaven; it is our friend in the desert, our society in solitude, our companion when friendless; it guideth us to happiness; it sustaineth us in misery; it is an ornament amongst friends, and an armour against enemies.

HADITH

FOR I have found that if a man were to write a book today he would on the morrow say: 'If this phrase were to be changed it would be better; if this other phrase were to be added it would improve the text; if this statement were introduced earlier it would be preferable, while if this other were omitted the text would be more beautiful.' In this reconsideration of one's work lies a great moral, and it is further proof that all men are imperfect.

AL-'IMAD AL-ISFAHANI, Editor

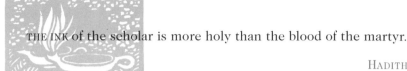

THE INK of the scholar is more holy than the blood of the martyr.

HADITH

KINGS GOVERN men, and learned men govern kings.

FOLK TRADITION, Wortabet

A FAVOURITE inscription over the portals of colleges in Arab Spain reads: 'The world is supported by four things only: the learning of the wise, the justice of the great, the prayers of the righteous, and the valour of the brave.'

CALLIGRAPHIC INSCRIPTION, Hitti

KNOWLEDGE, IT has been said, is not perfect without action; for knowledge is the tree, and action the fruit.

KALILA AND DIMNA, Knatchbull

K NOWLEDGE IS the life of humanity, spiritual practice is its conveyance, intellect is its ornament, and gnosis is its illumination and insight.

UMM AHMAD BINT 'A'ISHA, Cornell

EXTRACT GOLD from stone, and extricate pearls from the sea, and accept the good word from whomever speaks it.

FOLK TRADITION, *Editor*

THE MAN who is possessed of knowledge, is enabled by a corresponding line of conduct to reap the advantages of his acquirements; and he, who does not make a proper use of what he knows, is like the man, who in travelling chose a road in which he was aware that he should be exposed to danger.

KALILA AND DIMNA, *Knatchbull*

HOW MANY like us in the ages past
Have blindly soared, though like a pebble cast,
    Seeking the veil of mystery to tear,
But fell accursed beneath the burning blast?

AL-MA'ARRI, *Rihani*

THE WORST of men is a learned man who has not benefited from his learning.

FOLK TRADITION, *Editor*

KNOWLEDGE IS of three kinds: first, the knowledge of the Unity of God and this is common to all believers; second, knowledge gained by proof and demonstration, and this belongs to the wise and the eloquent and the learned; and third, knowledge of the attributes of the Unity, and this belongs to the saints, those who contemplate the Face of God within their hearts, so that God reveals Himself to them in a way in which He is not revealed to any others in the world.

DHU AL-NUN AL-MISRI, *Smith*

THE PRINCIPAL aim of a man in his pursuit of knowledge is to acquire what may be useful and profitable to himself ... when he has laid up a sufficient stock of learning to serve him on all occasions in his journey through life, it is then time for him to think of communicating the results of his experience and enquiries to his fellow creatures.

KALILA AND DIMNA, *Knatchbull*

EVERY AILMENT has a cure,
Except for stupidity – that has none.

FOLK TRADITION, *Editor*

THE ESSENCE of all wisdom is the fear of God.

FOLK TRADITION, *Editor*

KNOWLEDGE WILL be entrusted to neither the timid nor the
haughty.

FOLK TRADITION, *Howarth and Shukrallah*

WOE TO the ignorant man, when he has not learned even
once, and woe to the learned man when he has not put
into practice what he learned a thousand times!

AL-GHAZZALI, *Watt*

PEOPLE HARBOUR enmity against those things of which they are
ignorant.

'ALI IBN ABI TALEB, *Editor*

KNOWLEDGE IN the heart is not knowledge in books;
So be not infatuated with fun and play.
Memorize, understand, and work hard to win it.
Great labour is needed; there is no other way.

ABU HAMID AL-GHARNATI, *Makdisi*

SEEK KNOWLEDGE, for learning is a good deed before God; to disclose it is praise, to seek it is worship, to teach it is charity.

FOLK TRADITION, *Anonymous*

IN EDUCATION the life of the mind proceeds gradually from scientific experiments to intellectual theories, to spiritual feeling, and then to God.

KAHLIL GIBRAN, *Ferris*

ABOVE ALL, however, you must realize that the guidance which is the fruit of knowledge has a beginning and an ending, an outward aspect and an inward. No one can reach the ending until he has completed the beginning; no one can discover the inward aspect until he has mastered the outward.

AL-GHAZZALI, *Watt*

THE BEST of men is he who acquires learning but better than him is the one that transmits it.

FOLK TRADITION, *Editor*

POETRY AND LITERATURE

UNDERNEATH THE throne of God lie treasures the keys to which are
the tongues of poets.

HADITH

FOR THOUGH the moon of the heavens has set,
The full moon of poetry has arisen;
And though the moon of the eclipse has disappeared,
The full moon of eloquence has shone forth.

AL-HARIRI, *Preston*

BLOOD RELATIONSHIP we may lack,
But literature is our adopted father.

ABU TAMMAM, *Editor*

I SWEAR by God and His marvels,
By the pilgrims' rite and their shrine:
Hariri's *Assemblies* are worthy
To be written in gold each line.

AL-ZAMAKHSHARI, *Nicholson*

TIME IS but a reciter of my poems.
When I speak poetry, time itself becomes the singer
And those who march not energetically, my verse
Moves them to do so,
And he who has not learnt to sing, sings it resonantly.

AL-MUTANABBI, *Anonymous*

THESE 'MAKAMAT,' . . . contain serious language and
   lightsome,
      And combine refinement with dignity of style,
      And brilliancies with jewels of eloquence,
      And beauties of literature with its rarities,
Besides quotations from the 'Qur'an,' wherewith I
   adorned them,
And choice metaphors, and Arab proverbs that I
   interspersed,
      And literary elegancies, and grammatical riddles,
      And decisions upon ambiguous legal questions,
   And original improvisations, and highly wrought
      orations,
      And plaintive discourses, as well as jocose witticisms.

AL-HARIRI, *Gottheil*

WITHOUT HIGH virtues by poetry laid down
No glorious deed by man can be achieved.

ABU TAMMAM, Editor

MY DEEP poetic art the blind have eyes to see,
My verses ring in ears as deaf as deaf can be.
They wander far abroad whilst I am unaware,
But men collect them watchfully with toil and care.

AL-MUTANABBI, Nicholson

THE MEANS of reviving a language lie in the heart of the poet and upon his lips and between his fingers. The poet is the mediator between the creative power and the people. He is the wire that transmits the news of the world of spirit to the world of research. The poet is the father and mother of the language, which goes wherever he goes. When he dies, it remains prostrate over his grave, weeping and forlorn, until another poet comes to uplift it.

KAHLIL GIBRAN, Ferris

ART, CALLIGRAPHY AND THE PEN

PROCLAIM! AND thy Lord
Is Most Bountiful, –
He Who taught
(The use of) the Pen, –
Taught man that
Which he knew not.

QUR'AN 96: 3–5

THE PEN is the mind's ambassador, its most noble messenger, its most eloquent tongue, and its best interpreter.

ABU DAWOOD, *Editor*

THE PURPOSE of music, considered in relation to God, is to arouse longing for Him and passionate love towards Him and to produce states in which He reveals Himself and shows His favour... The heart's attainment of these states through hearing music is due to the mystic relationship which God has ordained between the rhythm of music and the spirit of man.

AL-GHAZZALI, *Smith*

THE ART of calligraphy is such that it can turn a plant into a rose and base metal into gold, and can sweeten the taste as well as purify the drink.

AHMED IBN ISMAIL, *Editor*

BAD CALLIGRAPHY is the disability of the man of letters.

FOLK TRADITION, *Editor*

CALLIGRAPHY IS essentially of the soul, even though it expresses itself in physical terms.

AL-NAZZAM, *Editor*

THERE IS no writer that shall not perish; but what his hand hath written endureth ever.
Write, therefore, nothing but what will please thee when thou shalt see it on the day of resurrection.

ARABIAN NIGHTS, *Lane*

Art, Calligraphy and the Pen ～ 229

THE REAL man is he who is apt in the art of calligraphy and knows how to swim.

FOLK TRADITION, *Editor*

FOR WRITING is a craft, and like all other crafts is conditioned by society.

This is why we find most nomads illiterate, while those among them who can read or write do so only imperfectly and hesitatingly. This, too, is why we find the art of calligraphy more developed in the more opulent towns, owing to a longer tradition in the craft, as in Cairo to-day.

IBN KHALDUN, *Issawi*

THE PEN is deaf but hears secret words, dumb but capable of speech, and without consciousness but aware of the reality of things.

FOLK TRADITION, *Editor*

THE PEN is a tree whose fruits are words, while thought is a sea whose pearls are wisdom.

FOLK TRADITION, *Editor*

ORATORY, ELOQUENCE AND THE POWER OF UTTERANCE

LET HIM who believes in God and the Day of Judgment either speak the good word or remain silent.

HADITH

A KIND word is like an act of charity.

FOLK TRADITION, Wortabet

A PERSON should not allow his words to admit of a wiser interpretation than he intended them to bear.

KALILA AND DIMNA, Knatchbull

THE BEST of all speech is that which uses few words, makes much sense and does not bore the listener.

FOLK TRADITION, Editor

THE TONGUE of man is one of the most active instruments of his ruin.

KALILA AND DIMNA, Knatchbull

FOR TRULY the excellence of man resides in two very small parts: the heart and the tongue.

FOLK TRADITION, Editor

PLAIN SPEECH is with the wise.

'ADI IBN ZAYD, Horovitz

ORATORY IS the cunning of the tongue over the ear, but eloquence is the joining of the heart with the soul.

KAHLIL GIBRAN, Ferris

A SHARP tongue cuts deeper than a sword.

FOLK TRADITION, Sabbagh

A MAN is hidden beneath his tongue.

'ALI IBN ABI TALEB, *Editor*

WE PRAISE thee, O God,
For whatever perspicuity of language thou hast taught us,
And whatever eloquence thou hast inspired us with,
    As we praise thee
  For the bounty which thou hast diffused,
And the mercy which thou hast spread abroad:
    And we pray thee to guard us
From extravagant expressions and frivolous superfluities
   ... And we beg thee freely to bestow
    Propitious succor to lead us aright,
    And a heart turning in unison with the truth,
    And a language adorned with veracity,
    And style supported by conclusiveness,
   And accuracy that may exclude incorrectness,
   And firmness of purpose that may overcome caprice,
   And sagacity whereby we may attain discrimination;
That thou wilt aid us by thy guidance unto right
   conceptions,

And enable us with thy help to express them with clearness,
And thou wilt guard us from error in narration,
And keep us from folly even in pleasantry,
So that we may be safe from the censure of sarcastic tongues,
And secure from the fatal effects of false ornament.

AL-HARIRI, *Preston*

HE WHO is sweet of tongue wins many friends.

'ALI IBN ABI TALEB, *Editor*

HEARTS ARE softened by the courteous messenger, but hardened by the coarse.

KALILA AND DIMNA, *Howarth and Shukrallah*

HE REMAINED silent for a long time, but when he spoke he uttered blasphemy.

FOLK TRADITION, *Editor*

HOW MANY a man seemed goodly to thee while he held his peace,
   whereof thou didst learn the more or less when he turned to speech.
The tongue is a man's one-half, the other, the heart within;
   besides these two naught is left but a semblance of flesh and blood.

ZUHAYR IBN ABI SULMA, *Lyall*

WORDS THAT wound are sometimes more painful than swords that pierce.

FOLK TRADITION, *Editor*

Oratory, Eloquence and the Power of Utterance

REASON AND SOUND JUDGEMENT

GOD HATH not created anything better than Reason, or anything more perfect, or more beautiful than Reason; the benefits which God giveth are on its account; and understanding is by it, and God's wrath is caused by disregard of it.

HADITH

A MAN of sound understanding is distinguished by eight different qualities; by courteous and affable behaviour, by a knowledge of himself, united with a strict and impartial observation of his own heart; by submission to lawful authority, and an endeavour to conciliate the good will of those who are in power; by great circumspection in his confidential communications; by becoming language and irreproachable conduct at the courts of kings; by secrecy, where his own interest is at stake, and fidelity in his engagements with others; by moderation in his discourse, so that no unpleasant consequence may arise from any hasty or intemperate word; and, lastly, by a prudent reserve and modest diffidence in delivering his opinion: and where these qualities are united in one person, ... they bring down blessings upon the head of him who possesses them.

KALILA AND DIMNA, *Knatchbull*

R EASON AND learning are like body and soul. Without the body, the soul is nothing but empty wind. Without the soul, the body is but a senseless frame.

KAHLIL GIBRAN, *Ferris*

OH! LET them in the marshes grope, or ride
Their jaded Myths along the mountain-side;
    Come up with me, O Brother, to the heights
Where Reason is the prophet and the guide.

AL-MA'ARRI, *Rihani*

A SPARROW would not offer molestation to a hawk, were it not for its folly, and the weakness of its sense.

ARABIAN NIGHTS, *Lane*

THE WISE man in prosperity feels ill at ease, while stupid fools in bitter days are never hard to please.

AL-MUTANABBI, *Editor*

HE WHO is deprived of understanding can neither distinguish what is praiseworthy from what is dishonourable, nor the good man from the bad.

KALILA AND DIMNA, Knatchbull

THE MOST profitable part of reason is that which makes known to you the grace of God towards you and helps you to give thanks for it and rises up to oppose sensuality.

AL-ANTAKI, Smith

WHEN REASON is complete, fewer become the words.

'ALI IBN ABI TALEB, Editor

WHEN GOD willeth an event to befall a man who is
endowed with reason and hearing and sight,
He deafeneth his ears, and blindeth his heart, and
draweth his reason from him as a hair.
Till, having fulfilled his purpose against him, He restoreth
him his reason that he may be admonished.

ARABIAN NIGHTS, Lane

INTELLIGENCE, GOOD sense, and caution are as necessary to man in his conduct through life, as the eye to vision, or the ear to the sense of hearing.

KALILA AND DIMNA, *Knatchbull*

THE INTELLIGENT and perfect man follows only the dictate of reason, and never continues in any state unless he feels free to do so for a definite reason and with a clear justification; he will not follow or obey or go along with his passion when it would lead him in a contrary direction.

AL-RAZI, *Arberry*

REASON IS the most excellent of God's gifts to man.

IBN 'AQIL, *Makdisi*

NOTHING CAUSES intellectuals to err except acts due to hastiness of temper and their being content with the Ancients to the exclusion of the Moderns.

IBN 'AQIL, *Makdisi*

Reason and Sound Judgement ✤ 239

ACKNOWLEDGEMENTS

In the preparation of this volume I have received much valuable help and advice from many generous friends and colleagues. My greatest debt is to Miss Sepedeh Hooshidari, who has been the chief coordinator of the whole project and without whose meticulous care and attention this anthology would not have been completed. I am also indebted to my students who not only helped me in choosing some of the material but have also spent many hours working with me on the final text: Mr James Madaio, Mr Siamak Majidi, Mrs Farinaz Firouzi Mehdi, Miss Poupak Moallem and Mr Hamed Yazhari. In addition, the following have contributed in various ways to this anthology: Miss Bita Farhoumand, Mr Basir van de Fliert, Mr Kalim Hanna, Mr Armin Mehdi and Mr Babak Mortazie.

To the following I owe profound thanks for the valuable advice they have given me, the books with which they have provided me, and the comments they have made on the introduction and the compilation as a whole: Dr Ihsan Abbas, Dr Miles Bradbury, Miss Fatma Essassi, Dr Shiva Akhavan, Mr William Collins, Dr Ismail Dahiyat, Mr Muhammad Ghuneim, Mrs Susan Halstead, Mr Mark Hellaby, Dr Raja'i al-Khanji, Dr Manaf Mansour, Mr Munzir Sleiman and Dr Sadek Sulaiman.

I would also like to thank the staff of Oneworld Publications – Victoria Warner, Rebecca Clare, Novin Doostdar, Helen Coward and Juliet Mabey – for all their hard work on this project.

Acknowledgement is hereby extended to the following for permission to reprint copyright material:

Alfred A. Knopf for permission to publish passages from *Love Songs of Asia* translated by Powys Mathers.

Ameen Rihani Organization for permission to publish passages from *The Luzumiyat of Abu al-ala al-Ma'arri* and *The Quatrains of Abu'l Ala* by Ameen Rihani.

American University of Beirut for permission to publish passages from *The Art of Badi az-Zaman al-Hamadhani As Picaresque Narrative* by James T. Monroe.

Anthony R. Ferris Estate for permission to publish passages from *Spiritual Sayings of Kahlil Gibran* by Kahlil Gibran, translated by Anthony R. Ferris; *Thoughts and Meditations* by Kahlil Gibran, translated and edited by Anthony R. Ferris; and *The Voice of the Master* by Kahlil Gibran, translated by Anthony R. Ferris.

E. J. Brill for permission to publish passages from *Qasida Poetry in Islamic Asia and Africa* edited by Stefan Sperl and Christopher Shackle.

Cambridge University Press for permission to publish passages from *The Poems of Al-Mutanabbi* translated by A.J. Arberry; *Arabic Poetry: A Primer for Students* by A.J. Arberry; *Aphorisms of the Statesman* (1961) translated by D.M. Dunlop; *The Cambridge History of Arabic Literature: 'Abbasid Belles-Lettres* (1990) Chapter 12, 'Love Poetry,' by A. Hamori and edited by Julia Ashtiany, T.M. Johnstone, J.D. Latham, R.B. Serjeant, and G. Rex Smith; *The Cambridge History of Arabic Literature: Arabic Literature to the End of the Umayyad Period* (1983) Chapter 20, 'Umayyad Poetry,' by Salma K. Jayyusi edited by A.F.L. Beeston, T.M. Johnstone, R.B. Serjeant, and G.R.

Smith; *Literary History of the Arabs* by Reynold A. Nicholson; and *Rabi'a the Mystic and Her Fellow Saints In Islam* (1984) by Margaret Smith.

Century Publishing for permission to publish passages from *A Winter in Arabia* by Freya Stark and *Southern Gates of Arabia: A Journey in the Hadramant* by Freya Stark.

City Lights Books for permission to publish passages from *Poems of Arab Andalusia* translated by Cola Franzen.

Clarendon Press for permission to publish passages from *The Letters of Abu al-'Ala'* translated by D.S. Margoliouth.

Copyright Clearance Center for permission to publish passages from *Journal of Arabic Literature* 'Seven Poems by Al-Hallaj' translated by Mustafa Badawi; and *The Poetry of Ibn Khafajah: A Literary Analysis* by Magda M. al-Nowaihi.

Cresset Press Limited for permission to publish passages from *A Mirror for Princes* by Kai Ka'us Ibn Iskandar and translated by Reuben Levy.

Edinburgh University Press for permission to publish passages from *Islam: Past Influence and Present Challenge* from the Chapter entitled 'The Pure Brethren and the Philosophical Structure of Their System' by Geo Widengren edited by Alford T. Welch and Pierre Cachia.

Ernest Benn Ltd. for permission to publish passages from *Told in the Market Place* translated by C.G. Campbell.

Fons Vitae for permission to publish passages from *Early Sufi Women* by Abu 'Abd ar-Rahman as-Sulami, edited and translated by Rkia Elaroui Cornell.

George Makdisi for permission to publish passages from *The Rise of Humanism in Classical Islam and the Christian West: With Special Reference to Scholasticism* and *The Rise of Colleges: Institutions of Learning in Islam and the West*.

Harper and Row for permission to publish passages from *Sufism: An Account of the Mystics of Islam* by A.J. Arberry.

Indian Council for Cultural Relations for permission to publish passages from *Contemporary Relevance of Sufism* 'Sufism and the Dignity of Man: Ibn 'Arabi and Rumi' by Masataka Takeshita and edited by Syeda Saiyidain Hameed.

Inner Traditions International for permission to publish passages from *The Book of Sufi Chivalry: Lessons to a Son of the Moment* by Muhammad ibn al-Husayn al-Sulami and translated by Sheikh Tosun Bayrak al-Jerrahi al-Halveti.

Islamic Foundation for permission to publish passages from *Al-Ghazali on the Duties of Brotherhood in Islam* translated by Muhtar Holland.

The Islamic Texts Society for permission to publish passages from *Seal of the Saints* by Michel Chodkiewicz and translated by Liadain Sherrard.

Jonathan Cape for permission to publish passages from *Travels in Arabia Deserta* by Charles M. Doughty.

John Murray for permission to publish passages from *Avicenna on Theology* translated by A.J. Arberry; *Spiritual Physick of Rhazes* translated by A.J. Arberry; *The Singing Caravan* by Henry Baerlein; *Antar: A Bedoueen Romance* translated by Terrick Hamilton; and *An*

Arab Philosophy of History: Selections from the Prolegomena of Ibn Khaldun of Tunis (1332–1406) translated and arranged by Charles Issawi.

Jubilee Printing and Publishing House for permission to publish passages from *The Renaissance of Islam* translated by Salahuddin Khuda Bakhsh and D.S. Margoliouth.

Kegan Paul International Ltd. for permission to publish passages from *Arabic Culture: Through Its Language and Literature* by M.H. Bakalla.

Luzac and Co. for permission to publish passages from *The Ring of the Dove* translated by A.J. Arberry; and *Readings from the Mystics of Islam* by Margaret Smith.

Longman Group Limited for permission to publish passages from *The Muslim Mind* by Charis Waddy.

Octagon Press for permission to publish passages from *Alchemy of Happiness* translated by Claud Field.

Omar S. Pound for permission to publish passages from *Arabic and Persian Poems* translated by Omar S. Pound.

Paulist Press for permission to publish passages from *Ibn al'Arabi: The Bezels of Wisdom* translated by R.W.J. Austin.

Pilot Press Limited for permission to publish passages from *Images from the Arab World: Fragments of Arab Literature Translated and Paraphrased with Variations and Comments* translated by Herbert Howarth and Ibrahim Shukrallah.

Phoenix Press for permission to publish passages from *Arabic-Andalusian Casidas* translated by Harold Morland.

Routledge and Kegan Paul Limited for permission to publish passages from *The Mystics of Islam* by Reynold A. Nicholson; *The Muqaddimah: An Introduction to History* Vol. 2 translated by Franz Rosenthal; *Travels in Asia and Africa* translated by H.A.R. Gibb, *A Dictionary of Arabic and Islamic Proverbs* edited by Paul Lunde and Justin Wintle.

Royal Asiatic Society for permission to publish passages from *The Table-Talk of a Mesopotamian Judge* translated by D.S. Margoliouth; and *The Tarjuman al-Ashwaq: A Collection of Mystical Odes* by Muhyi'ddin Ibn al-'Arabi and translated by Reynold A. Nicholson.

Sabbagh Management Corporation for permission to publish passages from *As the Arabs Say . . .* by Isa Khalil Sabbagh.

T.R. Press for permission to publish passages from greeting cards translated by G.B.H. Wightman and A.Y. al-Udhari.

Twayne Publishers, Inc. for permission to publish passages from *Introduction to Classical Arabic Literature* edited by Ilse Lichtenstadter.

University of Kentucky Press for permission to publish passages from *Dibil B. Ali* by Leon Zolondek.

For permission to reproduce the illustrations the publisher is indebted to the following:

Master Calligrapher Yasser Badreddin and *Dahesh Voice*, book jacket and pp. i, 81, 91, 101, 111, 217; Türk Kültürün Hizmet Vakfil p. 53; Kitabfurushi al-Shayar from Faza'ilu, Atlasi Khatt p. 179.

NB, every effort has been made to trace and acknowledge ownership of copyright. If any required credits have been omitted or any rights overlooked, it is completely unintentional.

BIBLIOGRAPHY

The Holy Qur'an

There are several translations of the Holy Qur'an in common use, not all of which are accepted by Muslim believers. I therefore consulted several Muslim authorities and was advised to use the translation of 'Abdullah Yusuf 'Ali. All passages quoted in this anthology are therefore from the following edition:

'Ali, 'Abdullah Yusuf (trans.) *The Holy Qur'an*. Beirut, Dar Al Arabia, n.d.

Hadith

There are several manuals of Hadith in translation. The following are the major sources which have been used in this anthology:

Ali, Maulana Muhammad *A Manual of Hadith*. Lahore, The Ahmadiyya Anjuman Ishaat Islam, n.d.

An-Nawawi, Muhyiuddin Abu Zakariyya *Riyadh as-Salihin*, trans by Muhammad Zafrullah Khan. London, 1989

Asad, Muhammad *Sahi Al-Bukhari vol. 5*. New Delhi, 1978

Bukhari, Muhammad bin Ismail *Sahi Al-Bukhari*, trans. Muhammad Muhsin Khan, 9 vols. Medina, 1973

Malik, ibn Anas *Muawatta,* trans. Muhammad Rahimuddin. New Delhi, 1981

Muslim, Abul Husain *Sahi Muslim*, trans. Abdul Hamid Siddiqi, 4 vols. Lahore, 1973–5

Shafi'i, Muhammad bin Idris *Risala*, trans. Majid Khadduri. Cambridge, 1987

al-Suhrawardy, Allama Sir Abdullah Al-Mamun (comp. and trans.) *The Sayings of Muhammad*. Boston: Charles E. Tuttle Company, 1992

Tabrizi, Shaikh Waliuddin Abdullah *Mishkat al-Masabih*, trans. J. Robson, 4 vols. Lahore, 1973

Main sources

In Arabic

In this section only authors and titles of Arabic works from which passages have been extracted are mentioned. It seems cumbersome and unnecessary to give the non-Arabic speaking reader all the bibliographical data as well.

Abu al-'Ali al-Qali, *Al-Amali*; Abu al-Faraj al-Isfahani, *Kitab al-Aghani*

Abu al-Hasan Ali al-Husayn Al-Masudi, *Muraj al-dhabab*; Abu'Ubaid al-Bakri, *Fasl al-Maqal Fi Sharh al-Amthal*; Ibn Abd Rabbih, *Al-Iqd Al-farid*; Ibn Khallikan, *Wafayat al-Ayan*; al-Maydani, *Majma 'al-Amthal*; al-Mubbashir Ibn Fatik, *Mukhtar al-Hikam wa Mahasin al-Kalm*; Ibn al-Nadim, *Al-Fihrist*; Ibn Qutaybah, *Uyun al-akhbar;*

Shihab al-Din Muhammad ibn Ahmad Al-Abshihi, *Al-Mustatraf Fi Kuli Fannin Mustazraf*; Thyrayya A. F. Malhas, *Al Qiyyam al-Ruhiyya Fi al-Shi'r al-'Arabi*; Yaqut al-Hamawi, *Irshad al-Arib*

In English

Abu-Tayeb. 'Rubaiyat Abu-Tayeb' trans. Amin Beder, *The Syrian World*, 5, 1931, p. 23

Al-'Arabí, Muhyi'ddín ibn *The Tarjumán al-Ashwáq: A Collection of Mystical Odes*, trans. R.A. Nicholson. London, Royal Asiatic Society, 1978

Ali ibn Abi Taleb *Maxims of 'Ali*. Lahore, Ashraf Publications 1963

Arberry, A.J. (trans.) *The Spiritual Physick of Rhazes*. London, John Murray, 1950

— *Sufism: An Account of the Mystics of Islam*. London, Allen & Unwin, 1950

— (trans.) *Avicenna on Theology*. London, John Murray, 1951

— (trans.) *The Ring of the Dove*. Luzac & Co., 1953

— *Arabic Poetry: A Primer for Students*. Cambridge, Cambridge University Press, 1965

— (trans.) *Poems of Al-Mutanabbí: A Selection with Introduction, Translation and Notes*. Cambridge, Cambridge University Press, 1967

Austin, R.W.J. (trans.) *Ibn al 'Arabi: The Bezels of Wisdom*. New York, Paulist Press, 1980

Badawi, Mustafa (trans.) 'Seven Poems by Al-Hallaj', *Journal of Arabic Literature*, 14, 1983, pp. 46–7

Baerlein, H. *The Singing Caravan*. London, John Murray, 1910

Bakalla, M.H. *Arabic Culture: Through Its Language and Literature*. London, Kegan Paul International Ltd, 1984

Bar-Hebraeus *Laughable Stories*, trans. E.A. Wallis Budge. Luzac & Co., London, 1897

Blunt, A. (trans.) *The Seven Golden Odes of Pagan Arabia: known also as the Moallaqat*, done into verse by Wilfred Scawan Blunt. London, Chiswick Press, 1903

Browne, E.G. *A Literary History of Persia vol. 2*. Cambridge, Cambridge University Press, 1956

— *A Literary History of Persia vol. 4*. Cambridge, Cambridge University Press, 1953

Campbell, C.G., (trans.) *Told in the Market Place*. London, Ernest Benn Ltd, 1954

Chenery, T. (trans.) *The Assemblies of al-Hariri vol. 1*. London, Williams and Norgate Ltd., 1867

Chodkiewicz, M. *Seal of the Saints: Prophethood and Sainthood in the Doctrine of Ibn 'Arabi*, trans. Liadain Sherrard. Cambridge, The Islamic Texts Society, 1993

Doughty, C.M. *Travels in Arabia Deserta*. London, Jonathan Cape, 1964

Dunlop, D.M., (trans.) *Aphorisms of the Statesman*. Cambridge, Cambridge University Press, 1961

al-Ghazzali, Abu Hamid Muhammad *Alchemy of Happiness,* trans. C. Field. London, Octagon Press, 1980

Gibran, K. *A Tear and a Smile*, trans. H.M. Nahmad. London, William Heinemann Ltd, 1972

— *The Voice of the Master*, trans. A.R. Ferris. London, Heinemann, 1973

— *Spiritual Sayings of Kahlil Gibran*, trans. and ed. A.R. Ferris. London, Heinemann, 1974

Hamilton, T. (trans.) *Antar: A Bedoueen Romance*. London, John Murray, 1819

Hamori, A. 'Love Poetry', in *The Cambridge History of Arabic Literature: 'Abbasid Belles-Lettres*, ed. J. Ashtiany *et al*. Cambridge, Cambridge University Press, 1990

Hitti, P.K. *History of the Arabs*. London, Macmillan Press Ltd, 1970

Holland, M. (trans.) *Al-Ghazali on the Duties of Brotherhood in Islam*. Leicester, Islamic Foundation, 1983

Howarth, H. and Shukrallah I. (trans.) *Images from the Arab World: Fragments of Arab Literature Translated and Paraphrased with Variations and Comments*. London, Pilot Press Ltd, 1944

Ibn Battuta *Travels in Asia and Africa* trans. H.A.R. Gibb. London, Routledge & Kegan Paul, 1926

Ibn al-Farid, Omar *Studies in Islamic Literature*, trans. R.A. Nicholson. Cambridge, University Press, 1921

Iskandar, Kai Ká'ús Ibn *A Mirror for Princes: The Qábús Náma*, trans. R. Levy. London, Cresset Press, 1951

Issawi, C. (trans. and arr.) *An Arab Philosophy of History: Selections from the Prolegomena of Ibn Khaldun of Tunis (1332–1406)*. London, John Murray, 1950

Jayyusi, S.K. 'Umayyad Poetry', in *The Cambridge History of Arabic Literature: Arabic Literature to the End of the Umayyad Period*, ed. A.F.L. Beeston et al. Cambridge, Cambridge University Press, 1983

Knatchbull, W. *Kalila and Dimna*. Oxford, W. Baxter, 1819

Lane, E.W. (trans.) *The Thousand and One Nights': Commonly called 'The Arabian Nights' Entertainments'*, vol. 1–4. New York, Nottingham Society, 1882

Lane-Poole, S. *Cairo: Sketches of its History, Monuments, and Social Life*. London, J.S. Virtue & Co., Ltd, 1898

Lichtenstadter, I. *Introduction to Classical Arabic Literature*. New York, Schocken Books, 1976

Lunde, P. and Wintle. J. *A Dictionary of Arabic and Islamic Proverbs*. London, Routledge & Kegan Paul, 1984

Lyall, C.J. *Translations of Ancient Arabian Poetry: Chiefly pre-Islamic*. London, Williams & Norgate, 1930

Makdisi, G. *The Rise of Humanism in Classical Islam and the Christian West: With Special Reference to Scholasticism*. Edinburgh, Edinburgh University Press, 1990

Margoliouth, D.S. (trans.) *The Letters of Abu al-'Ala'*. Oxford, Clarendon Press, 1898

— (trans.) *The Table-Talk of a Mesopotamian Judge*. London, Royal Asiatic Society, 1922

al-Masudi, *Historical Encyclopedia*. London, Oriental Translation Fund, 1841

Mathers, P. (trans.) *Love Songs of Asia*. New York, Alfred A. Knopf, 1946

Mez, A. *The Renaissance of Islam*, trans. Salahuddin Khuda Bakhsh and D.S. Margoliouth. Patna, Jubilee Printing and Publishing House, 1937

Mokarzel, S.A. (ed. and trans.) 'Worth of Knowledge', *The Syrian World*, 2, no. 3, September 1927, p. 10

Monroe, J.T. *The Art of Badi az-Zaman al-Hamadhani As Picaresque Narrative*. Beirut, American University of Beirut, 1983

Morland, H. (trans.) *Arabic-Andalusian Casidas*. London, Phoenix Press, 1949

Nicholson, R.A. *Translations of Eastern Poetry and Prose*. Cambridge, Cambridge University Press, 1922

— *The Mystics of Islam*. London, Routledge & Kegan Paul, 1963

— *A Literary History of the Arabs*. Cambridge, Cambridge University Press, 1969

al-Nowaihi, Magda M. *The Poetry of Ibn Khafájah: A Literary Analysis*. Leiden, E.J. Brill, 1993

Pound, O. (trans.) *Arabic and Persian Poems*. Washington, DC, Three Continents Press, 1986

Rihani, A. *The Luzumiyat of Abu al-ala al-Mu'arri*. New York, James T. White & Co., 1918

Rosenthal, F. (trans.) *The Muqaddimah: An Introduction to History, vol. 2*. London, Routledge & Kegan Paul, 1915

Sabbagh, Isa Khalil *As the Arabs Say . . .* Washington, DC, Sabbagh Management Corporation, 1983

Smith, M. *Readings from the Mystics of Islam*. London, Luzac & Co. Ltd, 1972

— *Rabia: The Mystic and her Fellow Saints in Islam*. Cambridge, Cambridge University Press, 1984

Sperl, S. and Shackle, C. (eds.) *Qasida Poetry in Islamic Asia and Africa*. Leiden, E.J. Brill, 1996

Stark, F. *A Winter in Arabia*. London, Century Publishing, 1983

— *The Southern Gates of Arabia: A Journey in the Hadramant*. London, Century Publishing Co., 1983

Steingass, F. (trans.) *The Assemblies of al-Hariri, vol 2*. London, Royal Asiatic Society, 1898

al-Sulami, Muhammad ibn al-Husayn *The Book of Sufi Chivalry: Lessons to a Son of the Moment*, trans. Sheikh Tosun Bayrak al-Jerrahi al-Halveti. New York, Inner Traditions International, 1983

as-Sulamí, Abu 'Abd ar-Rahmán *Early Sufi Women*, ed. and trans. R.E. Cornell. Louisville, KY, Fons Vitae, 1999

Takeshita, M. 'Sufism and the Dignity of Man: Ibn 'Arabi and Rumi', in *Contemporary Relevance of Sufism*, ed. Syeda Saiyidain Hameed. New Delhi, Indian Council for Cultural Relations, 1991

Waddy, C. *The Muslim Mind*. London, Longman Group Ltd, 1976

Warner, C.D. (ed.) *Library of the World's Best Literature: Ancient and Modern, vol. 2*. New York, J.A. Hill & Co., 1902

Watt, W.M. *The Faith and Practice of al-Ghazali*. Oxford, Oneworld, 1994

Welch, A.T., Cachia, Pierre. *Islam: Past Influence and Present Challenge*. Edinburgh, Edinburgh University Press, 1979

Wortabet, J. *Arabian Wisdom: Selections and Translations from the Arabic*. Lahore, Dutton & Co., 1968

Zolondek, L. *Dibil b. Ali*. Kentucky, University of Kentucky Press, 1961